D0990574

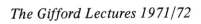

The Gifford Lectures 1971/72

The Nature of Mind

A. J. P. Kenny, *Balliol College, Oxford*
H. C. Longuet-Higgins FRS, *University of Edinburgh*
J. R. Lucas, *Merton College, Oxford*
C. H. Waddington FRS, *University of Edinburgh*

Edinburgh

at the University Press

© 1972
EDINBURGH UNIVERSITY PRESS
22 George Square, Edinburgh
ISBN   0   85224   235   2
North America
Aldine Atherton, Inc.
529 South Wabash Avenue, Chicago
Printed in Great Britain by
T. and A. Constable Ltd, Edinburgh

Contents

Preface

In May 1969 the Principal of Edinburgh University wrote to J. R. Lucas in these terms:

Dear Mr Lucas,

You will, I am sure, know what our Gifford Lectures are. In the past we have nearly always invited one lecturer to give a double series, that is to say, 10 lectures one year and 10 lectures the next year, and these are normally printed as a book.

The Gifford Committee, however, is disposed for the period 1971/72 and 1972/73 to try something different. Our idea, which is by no means fully formulated, is to persuade, if we can, four people to combine, giving perhaps five lectures each, with, we would hope, some joint seminars or disputations, the whole thing to be a developing concept. The general theme would be in the very broadest sense the development of mind, and we hope to start with a physical scientist, to move on with an animal behaviourist, or a psychologist, then some sort of philosopher, and finally a theologian.

We now have in the University as a Royal Society Professor someone who is, I believe, a friend of yours, namely Christopher Longuet-Higgins, who is much concerned nowadays with the physical basis of mind, and he has agreed to take part. We have just had a further meeting of the Committee with him, as a result of which we felt unanimously that we should like to ask you to be the theological participant. Although we had a number of ideas of biologists, psychologists, and philosophers of one sort or another, we didn't feel quite sure who would fit in best, and in the end we agreed that I should approach you to see whether you were in any way interested, and, if you were, further to invite you to get together with Christopher Longuet-Higgins and decide what other people you might like to rope in. . . .

Yours sincerely,
Michael Swann

The invitation was accepted, and before long the team was completed by the recruitment of A. J. P. Kenny, representing philosophy, and C. H. Waddington representing biology. The individual participants gave notice that they might step outside their allotted roles, as indeed they did when the time came. It was agreed to entitle the two-year series *The Phenomenon of Mind*; the title of the 1971/72 lectures would be *The Nature of Mind* and of the 1972/73 lectures *The Development of Mind*. This book is a record of the first of the two series; we plan to publish the second year's lectures in another volume.

For such a series there was little or no precedent, and we had to steer a careful course between formality and disorder. In the end it was decided that the standard form should be a prepared talk by one of the speakers, and a discussion opened by another who had studied the talk in advance. The remaining participants would then join in, but would not have seen the detailed text of the prepared talk, so that their reactions would be as spontaneous as those of the audience. This form was adopted for all except the first and last lectures of the series, and accounts for the change of literary style which will be apparent to the reader when he passes from the earlier to the later part of each chapter. (Each session was tape-recorded in its entirety, and editing has been kept to a minimum so as to preserve the informal atmosphere of the discussions, as when, for example, we addressed one another as 'Tony', 'Christopher', 'John' and 'Wad' respectively.)

In the first lecture each participant spoke for about 15 minutes, explaining the standpoint from which he approached the problems of mind, but there was no further discussion. The final lecture was also divided into four equal sections; each participant raised a particular topic for discussion, and the others added their comments and criticisms.

The Principal took the chair at a number of the lectures; others were chaired by Professor T. Torrance, Professor R. Hepburn, Professor J. McIntyre and Professor W. H. Walsh. We would like to thank them all for their tact and dexterity in dealing with such a motley crew.

A. J. P. Kenny
H. C. Longuet-Higgins
J. R. Lucas
C. H. Waddington.

First Lecture. Introduction

JOHN LUCAS

The nature of mind has been of perennial interest to philosophers, both as one of the characteristic features of man and as a precondition of all thought. Man has long been described, or even defined, as a rational animal, and even now biologists will allow that it is by his intelligence that man is distinguished from the other animals. Men are not only intelligent, they are also conscious beings who have feelings and emotions, who form opinions and intentions, who talk with one another, and sometimes show forth originality as well as often taking decisions and taking up positions, and occasionally seeking after truth.

There is a tradition of argument that to think clearly about the universe we have to take into account the fact that mental phenomena exist and that this betokens the existence of a mind that created the universe. Even in the more critical approach to philosophy that has been in fashion since the time of Hume, philosophy has still been concerned to secure a rational assessment of the intellectual powers of man; it has sometimes even been defined as thought about thought. I wouldn't go so far as to define it as that, but at least as a philosopher I must own that every philosopher, from Socrates to the Schoolmen and from Descartes to the present, has been and must be profoundly concerned with the nature of mind both because it is this that is peculiarly characteristic of human beings and because it is with this that we think. This we must consider if we are to come to terms with ourselves as being ourselves not merely men but thinking men, rational agents who reflect upon their own powers and their own aspirations.

It is not only, however, one of the perennial problems of philosophy but also now the matter of much more general and topical interest, and it is this that has led us to choose the phenomenon of mind as the general topic of the Gifford Lectures. The reason for this lies with the scientists, biologists, and computer engineers. We are all now aware that computer engineers can construct machines which are able to simulate many of the apparently intelligent and peculiarly human activities which we have hitherto regarded as our own preserve. Physiologists, especially neuro-physiologists, and psychologists have from a very different point of view been pressing home their enquiries about the nature of mind and seeking to provide scientific explanations of what had hitherto been

1

regarded as purely mental phenomena — one from which scientists should properly be excluded.

This has raised a number of problems and many people have felt that the development of scientific enquiry into the nature of mind has posed a threat to what we had hitherto regarded as the special preserve of morality and religion and the other things that we had held to be peculiarly human. And thus it is that we are at this time enquiring into the phenomenon of mind as something which is of concern from many different angles.

My own special interest in the nature of mind stems from my school-days when I was at Winchester and was listening to an essay by a much cleverer boy who was putting forward what he regarded as the scientific world-view, and maintaining that everything could be explained in terms of matter in strict categories of cause and effect. I didn't agree, but found it hard to resist his arguments till it occurred to me that the very fact that he was arguing with me and trying to secure my rational agreement to his position as being one that was true was itself an argument against the thesis that he was maintaining. The very fact that he addressed himself, as a rational agent, to me as another rational agent, belied his claim that everything could be completely explained in terms of the construction of his nervous system and the state of his endocrine glands.

When I went up to the University I pursued this argument further. I tried it on my tutor who immediately said that it was nonsense and that Russell's Paradoxes had shown that you couldn't ever hope to get an argument to bite its own tail, or to prove that another philosopher had sawn off the branch on which he was sitting. I was dismayed by this, although not entirely convinced, and then later heard of a very dim recherché mathematical theorem — Gödel's Theorem — somewhere near the foundations of mathematical logic, which seemed to do just what my tutor had told me I wasn't allowed to do. I pursued this argument and in the end I found a way of expressing in purely mathematical and logical terms the intuition I had had that arguments which cut off themselves from the branch on which they are sitting are in some way defective. I published this about ten years ago in an article and more fully last year in a book.

The conclusions were highly unwelcome to a number of people — I had the experience once at Massachusetts Institute of Technology of seeing an American frothing at the mouth, and it's often been maintained that I was morally very wicked to use metamathematical arguments to support moral conclusions. But although I have often been accused of wickedness and my arguments are highly unwelcome and many people disagree with me, 'their witness agreeth not with one another' and I am beginning to be fairly confident now that the argument itself cannot be faulted; not too confident

2

yet – who knows what might not turn up? But I am beginning – I mean my fingers are not as crossed as they were. And I think that in traditional terms this would lead me to say that although clearly now I wouldn't put forward the argument in exactly the same terms as when I was seventeen, the whole idea of materialism has rather evaporated. It seems very much more ethereal than it used to be in the days of schoolboy Newtonian mechanics and hard massy point particles. Nevertheless I think I would still like for this purpose to classify myself as holding some traditionalist position. Let me describe myself as a dualist, not in the sense that Descartes was – I am not a clever enough philosopher to handle even one substance, let alone two – nor in the more fashionable way now, as Strawson is, a dualist of predicates rather than of substances – I believe that P predicates and M predicates are different, but I am not logician enough ever to discover what the logical relations between them are. Rather let me say that I am a dualist with regard to *reasons*, and one of the arguments I shall put forward is that there is more than one (at least two) different type of reason, different type of explanation, different way of understanding.

To put it crudely now, I want to say that there are different ways in which we understand and explain the actions undertaken by a rational agent, and events which are caused by definite external conditions or causal factors. And if I can make good this argument it will have very great consequences both for science and for morality and religion. The old conflict between science and religion and the new conflict between science and humanity will be resolved by our coming to understand science as being very much more complicated than some scientists have hitherto felt impelled to say that in principle it was. Note the qualifications. Scientists have often been alarmed or angered by the attitude of moralists and philosophers and theologians who have put up a 'hands off' sign around man and around the mind. They have felt that it was entirely wrong to say that these things are inexplicable, and I shall not say that, but only that they are inexplicable within an extremely limited, restricted, and Procrustean scheme of explanation. I think scientists themselves will admit when they come to reflect upon what it is that they are doing that it embraces not one but many different types of explanation. And although I shall certainly maintain, in contrast to some traditional philosophers, that we can have a scientific investigation of the mind, and hope to explain mental phenomena, such an explanation will be such as not to threaten the mind, not to threaten our idea of humanity; instead of explaining it away, it will expound it in a way which is entirely compatible with our normal intuitions of freedom and responsibility and creativity, and the other peculiar characteristics which we have hitherto associated with the mind. That is to say, it will lead to

3

an enlargement of science rather than a reduction of mind.

This also will have great consequences for morality and for religion. It will reinstate what the moralists have long believed, the concept of an autonomous agent. We shall be able to explain men, we shall be able to explain their actions as the actions of beings who are themselves self-critical and who can make up their own minds what they are going to do. And it will also lead us to a very much wider understanding of the universe. We shall come (if we are to give a full understanding of the universe) to see it as to be explained not only in the rather limited categories which were put forward originally by David Hume, but with a much more generous idea of rationality and what it is to count as an explanation; that is, we shall reckon that if we are to give a full understanding of the universe, we must enlarge our categories of explanation and rationality to be able to accommodate the evident fact that there are minds which exist in the universe, and we shall explain these in terms of a wider view of rationality, which, according to the opening verses of St John's Gospel is but another name for God.

LONGUET-HIGGINS

It would be perverse to disagree with many of the things that John Lucas has said about the mind, and in particular his insistence upon its rationality as one of its essential characteristics. Nonetheless I feel dissatisfied with his philosophical approach, which seems to take us hardly any further towards a real understanding of the nature of mind. Not that there is anything shameful about old-fashioned methods of intellectual enquiry if one cannot improve upon them, but can we afford, in discussing mental phenomena, to disregard the lessons and insights which can be gleaned from modern psychology, logic and linguistics? Perhaps we could, if psychology were no more than the observation of people's behaviour, if logic were simply the idle manipulation of symbols, and if linguistics were no more than a sophisticated word game. And it must be admitted that some practitioners of these arts have done little to correct such impressions. But what inspired the founders of logic, psychology, and linguistics? The belief, surely, that the only way to advance in our understanding of the mind beyond the stage of metaphysical generalities was to attend closely to the actual phenomena which we take to be evidence of mental activity and to try to interpret these phenomena by the construction of models – or, if you prefer, of scientific theories. I use the word 'scientific' with caution because it may give a wrong impression, which I shall immediately do my best to dispel.

The word 'science' has had a chequered history. Originally, it was a synonym for knowledge or understanding, but it soon became a label for that part of our knowledge which was

4

acquired by experiment or observation and could be fitted together into a logically coherent structure. Scientific facts not only had to be publicly verifiable: they had to be amenable to interpretation. And scientific theories not only had to fit the facts; they had to make assertions which were open to experimental disproof. Knowledge meeting these stringent conditions was found to yield enormous power over the natural world, and the word 'science' has now gained such emotional and technological overtones that its primary meaning has been almost forgotten. But it is the best word we have for describing the interpretation of natural phenomena, and I propose to use it in this sense in spite of the risk of misunderstanding. In short, I shall suggest that for coming to grips with mental phenomena metaphysical generalities are not enough. We must try to be as rigorously scientific in our approach to the problems of mind as to the problems of matter.

Again, there will be misunderstandings unless I try to forestall them. Only the most simple-minded scientist, it will be asserted, can believe that it is possible to do science without making any metaphysical assumptions, and his science will inevitably be coloured by his metaphysical presuppositions. There are various possible replies to this criticism of science without metaphysics, or at least without an explicit metaphysic. One is to point to the wide agreement between scientists of entirely different cultural backgrounds on both experimental and theoretical issues. Another is to observe what happens when scientific theories are called in question on metaphysical grounds. Four examples come to mind. Wilberforce's attack on Darwin's Theory of Evolution ended in a rout. The attempt by Lysenko to re-establish, on quasi-Marxist principles, the inheritance of acquired characteristics did untold damage in Russian biology. Metaphysical preconceptions about the essential distinctness of space and time have obstructed, and still obstruct, a clear appreciation of what is asserted in the theory of relativity and have even led some intransigent philosophers of science to question the integrity of their scientific colleagues. And fourthly, the Quantum theory, which underpins the whole of physics, is still being sniped at because its laws, though they have survived the most searching tests, remain uninterpretable within metaphysical schemes which insist on the objective reality of all physical situations.

To put the matter in this way is to oversimplify, insofar as the construction of scientific theories is a never-ending process involving assertions which at one time may seem to be merely metaphysical but later are seen to hold empirical implications. And nothing in science could be more provisional at the present time than our ideas about the mind and how to study it.

5

Tomorrow afternoon I shall indeed be severely critical of some present scientific thinking about mental phenomena and will suggest that there are some serious categorial confusions which at present bedevil the study of the brain, which is the seat of our own mental activity. Indeed, I would not be taking part in these discussions unless I felt, with the other participants, that we are very unlikely to achieve a better understanding of the mind without a thorough examination in philosophical terms of the concepts that will be needed for building a properly scientific theory. But of one thing I feel certain: we shall not succeed, nor will others, by taking up fixed metaphysical positions in advance. By all means let us attempt to state as clearly as we can those issues to which we feel that a theory of the mind must address itself, and until we have a satisfactory theory these issues will have to be couched in the language of philosophy rather than in the language of science. And by all means, if we can, let us look around to see whether there are any overriding limitations to which any theory of the mind must conform. Perhaps, as John Lucas will later argue, the undecidability of arithmetic puts paid to a particular type of psychological theory, though I very much doubt it. But if there are any limiting principles of this kind to be discovered, then their discovery promotes them from the realm of metaphysical prohibitions to the status of scientific assertions, and they become part of psychology in its proper sense.

To me, the most significant question about the mind is 'How are we to set about constructing a satisfying theoretical account of mental phenomena?' I suppose that each one of us is expected to show his hand on this occasion, if only to raise expectations of what disputes are likely to arise between us. I, for better or for worse, am professionally committed to the study of cognitive processes. The question has actually arisen in this university as to whether my colleagues and I are psychologists or not. The issue is confused by a schism in psychology itself. Is it legitimate for a psychological theory to include 'subjective' concepts such as motive, decision and interpretation, or must psychology be limited to the discussion of overt behaviour in terms of measurable stimuli and responses? If the latter, then cognitive psychology is a non-subject and I am a non-scientist. Naturally, I like to think otherwise. But then the question arises: in what form are we to cast the theory of mind which has room for genuinely mental phenomena? Freud made a serious attempt to do this, and though his theories certainly lacked mathematical precision, perhaps mathematical precision is not everything. But in this second half of the twentieth century the engineers and mathematicians have presented us with a machine which challenges us to think in a new way about our intellectual processes – the electronic computer. If we can ask and answer questions about how computers do arithmetic, why should we not ask the same questions about ourselves, and hope ultimately for as detailed an answer? And if the question can be asked about arithmetic why should we not ask it about our less pedestrian intellectual activities? It would be sheer negligence not to see what light can be thrown on the nature of mental processes by comparing them with the various steps in a computation; and this, in my opinion, is by far the most interesting possibility which the computer has opened before us. To do so is not to make any extravagant claims for computers or to blaspheme against the humanity of man. Not to do so would be a far worse insult, suggesting that we human beings could not stand critical comparison with our own inventions.

KENNY

Longuet-Higgins has just said that philosophy cannot take us very far in the study of the mind. The question must have occurred to many of you 'what can philosophy have to say at all about the phenomenon of mind?' In the nineteenth century, when philosophy in these islands was dominated by the spirit of Hegel, the answer might well have been 'everything'. Philosophy consisted essentially of logic and metaphysics. Logic was the study of the laws of thought and metaphysics was the understanding of the universe as the evolution of spirit. In the present century, since experimental psychology has become an independent discipline, the answer which springs to mind is likely to be 'nothing'. Mind as spiritual entity has been exploded. The study of mind, if it is not to be superstitious mystification, must be either the study of behaviour or the study of brain. The study of behaviour is best done by the psychologist and perhaps the sociologist; the study of brains is for the biochemist and neurophysiologist: in neither area is there any scope for the arm-chair intuitions of the philosopher.

Now if either of these views were true there would be no room for the four of us on this platform. If the Hegelian view were the true one then John Lucas and I should have it to ourselves; if the contrary view were true we shouldn't be here at all. I believe that the truth lies between the two extremes, so that we can all sit down together.

I'd agree with Longuet-Higgins that metaphysical generalities will not take us far, though I am not quite happy with Lysenko and Wilberforce as the spokesmen of metaphysical generalities. But I'll try to explain what I think is the true role of the philosopher in these matters. It is certainly not the thing that Longuet-Higgins dislikes most, the taking up of metaphysical positions in advance of the evidence.

In the last century not only psychology but also logic has set up house independently of philosophy. It has become highly mathematical. Its contemporary practitioners no longer think of it as the study of the laws of thought, if by laws of thought we mean natural laws which govern our thinking in the way in which Newton's laws govern motion. If we are to think of the truths of logic as laws at all, the laws to which we should compare them are the laws which regulate the operation of traffic – laws which notoriously differ from those which describe the actual behaviour of traffic. We differ from the Hegelians, then, over the nature of logic. Few philosophers today would accept a Hegelian metaphysic either. Few, I mean, would see the study of the world as a whole as the study of the manifestation of mind. Some philosophers, of course, continue to believe that the world was created by God and in that way is a product of intelligence. However, I think even theistic philosophers would not wish to rest their claim to contribute to the study of the human mind on their theistic beliefs alone. What then do philosophers have to contribute, and on what is their contribution based?

It's a familiar jibe that philosophers only say what everybody knows, in language that nobody can understand. Now I think that it is true that the starting point of philosophy is what everyone knows, but it is a well-known fact that half of what everyone knows is true, and the other half is false. The aim of the philosopher is to give explicit and precise formulation to our common, informal, hazy, vital and passionate beliefs about ourselves and about the world in such a way that we can coolly and self-consciously sort out the truth from the prejudice in what we all know. Styles and methods of philosophy differ from age to age, but I think that this job is clearly the common aim of the question-and-answer games which Socrates used to play, of the metaphysical doubtings of Descartes and of the investigations into everyday idiom which until recently used to be the common practice of philosophers at Oxford.

Now in the particular area of philosophy of mind it is particularly important to make explicit and criticise what we all believe we know. Our intuitions about fundamental physics are not likely to be at all strong and they are almost certainly of no value, but when we turn to the study of mind we turn to an area in which we are all convinced that we have a special title to speak. If I don't know what the contents of my own mind are (each of us feels) then who does? Few of us claim to be any sort of expert in any of the sciences of mind, but each of us feels that even if he is not in possession of the expertise of the science of mind at least he is the intimate and irreplaceable custodian of its data. To sort out what is true from what is false in this conviction is itself one of the central tasks of the philosophy of mind. It seems to me that it is a task to which experimental psychology, too, cannot be indifferent.

8

One way in which men have tried to express their special relationship to their own minds is this. Each one of us, we feel, has in addition to his public bodily history another inward life in which there occur events which are private to him, of which he alone is a witness, and of which others can know only by his testimony. This position is often called a dualist position, since it regards body and mind as two distinct entities. Many people, I think, would say that that's just what the word 'mind' means, namely a private and inward realm of this kind, and they may say this whether they are dualists who affirm the existence of an inner realm or they are behaviourists who deny the existence of mind.

Now I believe that this supposition is incorrect and has been shown to be such by the patient work of Wittgenstein. His later philosophy of mind I take to be one of the most interesting philosophical events of the century, and the importance of his work is that it shows a third way between the unacceptable alternatives of dualism and behaviourism. According to the dualist, the relation between mental processes and their expression in behaviour is a contingent relation; it is not any sort of logical necessity. Mind and body are separate; each of them could in principle live its life independent of the other. For the behaviourist, on the other hand, if he is prepared to give meaning to the word 'mind' at all, then the relation between mind and body is in some way a necessary identity – all ascriptions of mental attributes to human beings, if they are not to be mere myth-making, must be reducible to ascriptions of bodily behaviour whether actual or hypothetical. Wittgenstein argued against both these schools of thought. He thought that bodily behaviour was neither identical with, nor merely contingently connected with, the mental life of which it is the sign. Bodily behaviour isn't identical with mental life; it is only the sign of it, it is only evidence for it. But this evidential relation is one which is built into the meaning of the mental predicates which we use of human beings; it isn't something which is discovered by induction and experiment.

From this point of view both dualism and behaviourism share a common false presupposition – namely that of the essential privacy of mental events. The dualist argues like this: mental events are essentially private; science cannot study what is essentially private; therefore there can be no science of mental events. The behaviourist argues: science can study the whole life of man, science cannot study what is essentially private; therefore the life of man does not include mental events. Both conclusions, I think, are false; both arguments depend on one true premise – namely, science cannot study what is essentially private – and one false premise: mental events are essentially private. Wittgenstein's merit was to show that the second premise was false and the true premise was harmless. The reason why science cannot study what is essentially private is that the essentially private is a piece of philosopher's nonsense.

This then is the first way in which the philosopher can hope to contribute to the study of the phenomenon of mind. Philosophy of mind can help to sort out what is the truth and what is the muddle in what we all think we know about our own minds. Though this is not an empirical investigation it is not a matter of indifference to the empirical investigator, for it concerns the correct identification and description of the data which he hopes to systematise and explain. However, it is not only the philosophy of mind but also the philosophy of language which can cast light on the phenomenon of mind. For if we are to study the nature of mind by studying its manifestations in behaviour, it is clear that the study of linguistic behaviour will be of paramount importance in the investigation of specifically human intelligence. If we look on human beings as systems whose output is to be explained in terms of input and internal organisation, the most important part of that output will be the linguistic output, and if we are to begin to account for the output we must be clear about its nature. And here again recent developments in philosophy can help, for along with the development of formal logic and the re-invigoration of philosophy of mind, the greatest progress in philosophy in recent decades has been in the philosophy of language.

For the past decade and more, philosophers and experimental psychologists have both been studying, with a growing degree of mathematical sophistication, the syntax and semantics of natural languages. During this period their work has brought them closer and closer together on terrain which was traditionally occupied by the linguist. No doubt the philosopher approaches this area from an *a priori* viewpoint and the psychologist from an experimental one. But in this area the boundary between conceptual and empirical elements is more than usually difficult to draw. In a later lecture I hope to offer some suggestions as to where it should be drawn. But the difficulty of drawing it makes the philosopher still indispensable to the study of man as a language-using animal.

But is it after all only the use of language which makes man unique — if he is unique? If linguistic intelligence is merely the ability to carry out formal operations of a certain complexity, for instance the parsing of sentences or the proof of theorems in a formal system, then it seems clear that linguistic intelligence is a comparatively unimportant part of humanity and that it is shared by inert artifacts like computers. It is rather in the interpretation of formal systems, their application to the world and to our concerns, that we really display the powers of mind, and from this point of view formal systems are simply games we play and tools we use. Computers, like Humean reason, are, and should only be, the slaves of our passions. Where they fall short of human beings is not so much in lacking intelligence but in lacking passions. Of course, reason itself includes more than Hume thought; rationality involves not only powers of the intellect but attitudes of the will. To be rational is to be capable of acting for reasons, and reasons include both cognitive and affective factors — purposes as well as information.

If I had to single out what makes man unique I would even today want to start from Aristotle's definition of man in the Nichomachean Ethics — where he defines man not as a rational animal but as a choosing agent, that is to say an agent whose actions are the result of willing wedded to thought and thought wedded to will. By will Aristotle meant decisions based on long-term goals which were self-selected. It is this, it seems to me, which computers lack. Only an agent such as Aristotle describes is capable of conferring meaning on formal systems, is capable of making signs into symbols. For meaning cannot be defined without intention and knowledge and the operations of non-living hardware only have meaning because of the intentions of their human agents. That is a thought which I hope to develop next week.

What Aristotle's definition leaves out, it seems to me, is the element of creativity. Creativity seems the third principle characteristic of the human mind, besides intelligence and rationality. Creativity is the hardest to define and I shall not attempt to do so — but in some ways it is the most important. For we share linguistic intelligence with computers and we share passions and purposes with other animals, so that if the Aristotelian account is adequate then we differ from animals only because of what we share with computers, and we differ from computers only because of what we share with animals. Creativity is the characteristic which, if any does, separates us both from inert artifacts and from brute beasts.

WADDINGTON
The previous three speakers have outlined — illuminated — the stage on which most of our discussions of the human mind are going to take place, largely in the context of linguistic expression and by comparison with some of the performances of computers. They are all professional students of these topics: two professional philosophers, one professional — well, he wasn't quite sure whether he would allow himself to be called a theoretical psychologist or what. But I am afraid I am speaking from right outside this topic. I am not a professional student of the human mind at all. I am a straight biologist. I think my function here is to provide — or at least suggest — some of the background, let me call it, against which the human mind can, and I think should, be seen.

One must first ask 'In what circumstances would we use the

11

word "mind" in biology?' Any circumstances that would suggest that we should use it would certainly involve an animal behaving in some way in response to certain inputs of stimuli. If its behaviour was an exceedingly simple reaction to a stimulus, such as for instance a knee jerk when you hit the right tendon, I think we wouldn't want to use the word 'mind'. We are tempted to use the word 'mind' when we know that something is going on in the nervous system and that it is something very complex. Perhaps it need not necessarily be only in the brain, but in most of the higher animals it is mainly in the brain. When things go on in the brain stem, I am not certain whether we would be tempted to call them 'mind' or not.

So, in the first place, I am making the point that there is an area of indecision as to what things we would include in the 'mind', and what things we would not.

Granted that there are some very highly complex phenomena in the central nervous system which we might be tempted to call 'the mind', can we go any further than that? First of all, I would like rather to rule out, for purposes of this discussion, the idea that we can deduce much about the nature of these complex phenomena that we call mind from our understanding of the processes of evolution by which they have been produced. We realise, of course, that the higher organisms have been brought into being by evolution, and that it is evolutionary processes which have shaped their physical being and their mental apparatus. But, in my opinion, our knowledge of the theory of evolution is very very much less than is usually alleged, and is certainly not enough to enable us to deduce anything much about the nature of the mind. Any very complex process in animals, such as we have said that mind must be, must depend on a very large number of hereditary factors. It can perhaps be stopped by an inappropriate signal, an inappropriate factor, in the animal's hereditary constitution, but it cannot be created by any single factor – it must depend on the interactions of a very large number of factors. Merely to say that this aspect of the animal's physical or mental constitution is determined by its heredity doesn't really tell you anything very interesting about it. It is like saying it is made up of atoms. Of course – so what?

Another analogy one might use is that the individual genes determining the heredity of an animal may perhaps be compared to the stones forming the aggregate in a concrete structure. You can't discuss much of the difference between a concrete building by Corbusier and Candela, say, by discussing the aggregates they used in the concrete. Of course, the aggregates are absolutely essential – they could not get along without stones in the concrete – and if some of the stones are really made of weak clay it will make a defective structure, and so on. But the things you are really interested in in the buildings are not dependent on the aggregate, but on properties of the much larger members into which the aggregates are formed. The same thing seems to me to be true of the complex organs of higher organisms, and certainly true of such complicated phenomena as the mental events which we call 'mind'.

Similarly, simply to say that a certain type of output from an animal is 'instinctive' doesn't add anything much to a discussion of mind. In an excessively simple instinctive action, when an animal simply responds in a defined way to a defined stimulus, one might say there is very little mental activity involved in that. But other types of instinctive behaviour involve much more complex outputs. For instance, consider a bird building a nest — if you take a bird that builds a nice complex nest, like a weaver bird, say, that is instinctive behaviour; birds of one species will always build a nest of a certain pattern. But it must be a highly complex nervous activity, as you will realise if you imagine youself approaching a nest, carrying a piece of straw in your beak, and trying to decide how to weave it into the nest. This is, it seems to me, behaviour worthy of being called mental, although it is also 'instinctive'.

Can we say that mental behaviour must always be conscious behaviour? This raises the question which Kenny was speaking about, of the private world of consciousness — I don't want to argue at the moment just how private the world of consciousness is — it's certainly pretty private as between myself and the chimpanzee or dog or cat. I just can't tell what, if anything, they are conscious of. I am going to suggest that from the biological point of view of mind consciousness is not necessarily terribly important. Nearly everything that we usually do with conscious thought, we can actually do, without conscious thought. For instance, we are not normally conscious of the very involved mental nervous events that must be going on controlling our movements. Even in some of the higher forms of movement: can one really say that a concert pianist is actually conscious of putting down particular fingers on particular notes when he is playing a fast passage? Or is a good ball player really conscious of exactly what he is doing to that ball? It seems to me in neither case is he fully conscious. He is conscious that he wants to produce a certain effect, and he is conscious of the effect he is actually getting, but not conscious of the actual nervous steps, or even the physical steps, involved in the process. Similarly, as we all know, many people have said that some of their major discoveries, of a really creative kind, have as it were leapt into their mind after a good night's sleep, or something like that, but they have not been conscious of the mental processes by which they worked out what eventually turn out to be highly complex and logical structures.

13

And this comes out also, I think, if we consider the relation of language to mind. Now we are certainly going in the next few days to have a great deal of discussion of language in this series of lectures, and I think we will find — I am not a professional in this field — that the analysis of language has given us a lot of clues to the ways in which mental processes may be working. But I think the mental processes can often work without the language; the language may be indicative evidence, but it is not, I should suggest, a necessary part of the process. I would like to quote what Einstein once wrote about his thought processes. He said: 'The words of the language as they are written or spoken do not seem to play any role in my mechanism of thought. The psychical entities which seem to serve as elements in thought are signs and more or less clear images which can be voluntarily reproduced and combined. The above-mentioned elements are, in my case, of visual and some of muscular type. Conventional words or other signs have to be sought for laboriously only as the secondary stage, when the mentioned associative play is sufficiently established and can be reproduced at will'. That is the testimony of a very profound thinker, saying that language is not necessarily the accompaniment of activities which one is bound to call mental. The biologist is essentially interested in another question that has also been raised, particularly by Longuet-Higgins, I think; when can mental activity be said to be intelligent?

Activity can be mental without necessarily being intelligent. I think what one means when one calls the activity intelligent is that it produces some successful result; and by 'successful' the biologist would, in the first place, think of success in terms of natural selection. Now natural selection is a much more complex process than is usually suggested by elementary discussions of biology. They often confine it to 'leaving a lot of off-spring'. Now leaving a lot of off-spring is quite a successful thing to do in some cases, but not if you leave so many that you eat yourself out of your hearth and home, as the human race seems to be in some danger of doing at the present time. Natural selection is really concerned with selecting things which have long-lasting stability — which can go on lasting for many, many generations. It is quite a complex topic, to which I shall hope to return in a later lecture. But in biology, then, intelligent behaviour would be behaviour that is successful in achieving one of the objectives of the organism concerned. You cannot define intelligence without bringing in a reference to a goal or objective. In nature such goals and objectives may be set up by the operation of natural selection, and they may be quite complex; we will discuss later what some of those complexities are. But, of course, man has certainly the possibility not only of having his goal set for him by natural selection, but of defining and

14

setting his own goals. How far other animals can do this is not quite so easy to say, but I think we could certainly assert that man is capable of setting his own goals and this settles what he means by 'intelligent'.

Is this, perhaps, the essential distinction between mankind and the computers, of which we are going to be told in more detail? Normally man sets the goals for his computers. He fixes his computer to carry out operations, working on inputs similar to the language inputs to his own mind, and producing an output related to some goal that he has set the computer to do. If that were all that computers could ever do, then they would always be the slaves of human passions – to use Kenny's phrase. And there would be an absolute distinction between mankind and his artifacts in that man sets his own goals and he sets goals for his artifacts. I am, however, sufficient of a believer, if you like, in 'natural theology', which I think is the subject of the Gifford Lectures, to be not quite certain that computers couldn't conceivably do something better than that. I tend to believe that the goals of mankind are not arbitrarily invented but are actually inherent in the nature of the universe. I don't say man has really succeeded very often in finding them, but it seems to me that his great endeavour is the attempt to discover what goals are fixed by the nature of the universe, and the nature of himself living within it. If this is so, then it is not inconceivable that a computer equipped with sense organs and so on, could examine the world as we examine the world, and deduce from it the same sort of goals that we deduce from it. It would seem to me that if you could get a computer to do that, and only if you could get a computer to do that – to examine the world and to formulate for itself appropriate goals which would in effect be the passions that Kenny was referring to – only if it could do that could you really say that computers had become intelligent.

Now I leave this as a challenge to Longuet-Higgins. If he thinks he is ever going to be able to assemble such a computer, I think he would probably like to postpone the date for its birth some little time into the future.

Second Lecture. The Failure of Reductionism

It has fallen to me to open the bowling for the sciences, at the risk of being hit for six by Kenny, who is to be opening batsman for the humanities. Unfortunately, I shall not be able to do what might be expected of me by Lucas, which is to assert that everything except matter is immaterial — if he will excuse the pun. But I suppose I shall have to expound that view, if only to improve upon it, which is what I want to do in this lecture. In brief, I propose to examine the doctrine of scientific reductionism, to give reasons why I regard it as untenable, and to drop some hints as to what will actually have to be done by scientists, and is already being done, if we are to create a worthy science of the mind, rather than being condemned to mechanistic platitudes on the one hand, and philosophical exhortations on the other.

The reductionist position, as I see it, takes several forms, varying in sophistication. The confident young scientist described last time by Lucas, had obviously been impressed by the beauty and order of modern physics, and by its apparent ability to give a coherent account of all the phenomena — or nearly all — manifested by matter in motion. Objects as different as the sun and the moon, substances as different as chalk and cheese, influences as obscure as magnetism and X-rays, could all — or so it seemed — be brought within the compass of the physical sciences, and made comprehensible in terms of a small number of basic concepts and fundamental constants of nature. It was a heady experience, calculated to provoke a conversion to the view immortalised in Rutherford's famous dictum 'There is physics, and there is stamp collecting'. There were, of course, many matters of detail which had not been fully cleared up. One could state with great accuracy the laws describing the motion of a falling apple, but people hadn't yet explained exactly how a pip grew into a Cox's Pippin. Living organisms were certainly very different in their observable behaviour from crystals, atoms, and bar magnets. But as far as one could tell, the laws of conservation of mass and energy, and even the second law of thermodynamics, applied with equal force to living and non-living matter. The organic chemists had already synthesised many of the complex molecules which are formed in the tissues of plants and animals, and vitalism had been rudely expelled from polite scientific society. What better proof could there be of the overriding supremacy of the physical sciences and their ultimate ability to illuminate the whole universe of our experience?

So much for the Zeitgeist from which naive reductionism has sprung, at least in my own generation, though I suspect that the pendulum is now swinging rapidly in the opposite direction. But what is the intellectual content of this position, as opposed to its emotional symptoms?

The starting point of the reductionist argument is the supremacy of physics, the doctrine that any assertion which carries implications about the properties of matter must either conform with the laws of physics or be discarded. Let me illustrate this entirely reasonable view with one or two examples. First, suppose someone asserted that by taking thought he could determine his velocity of motion through space. Would we take him seriously? Of course not. Why? Because one thing which we know for certain now about space and time is that absolute motion is not only impossible to detect but impossible to define, if we take seriously, as we must, the experiments and the reasoning on which relativity is based. My second example is clairvoyance, the claim to be able to perceive future events. At the heart of physics is the causality restriction: if two events are in a relation of temporal precedence, then causal influences cannot be propagated from the later one to the earlier one. If anyone is genuinely clairvoyant, then modern physics is fundamentally in error. There are no two ways about it. Finally, to anticipate our discussions on free-will and determinism, does Heisenberg's principle of uncertainty represent a gap in physics, through which we can escape from the tyranny of physical determinism? No, says the physicist. The principle of indeterminacy is a principle of impotence. Unless quantum mechanics is all wrong, *no-one* can predict the way an excited electron will jump, or explain why it jumped the way it did, in terms of antecedent circumstances. So if an electron in my head jumps in a certain direction when I make a free choice, I cannot afterwards account for the way it jumped by referring to my choice, or in any other way either. It would, in any case, seem very odd to advance such an explanation for a physical event — a point to which we shall doubtless return in our later discussions.

Now, perhaps, we are in a better position to state the doctrine of scientific reductionism, and to see what important questions, if any, it leaves unanswered about the nature of mind. It is, in a sense, a natural extension of scientific materialism, if that label is taken to signify a rejection of any concept which cannot be directly related to the world of things and stuff. Reductionism makes a less sweeping claim. The laws of physics, which carry the ultimate authority about the material world, are taken to be irreducible. The reductionist recognises, however, that there are other sciences, such as chemistry, which have almost as high standards of generality and precision, and that these must find a place in the scientific

17

scheme. But he notes with satisfaction that, after many centuries of illusory independence, chemistry has been fitted into the framework of physics, at least in principle. As Paul Dirac remarked in the first chapter of his book on quantum mechanics, the whole of chemistry and a large part of physics could in principle be explained by the new theoretical discoveries. So chemistry, the reductionist claims, is really physics, and, furthermore, biology is really chemistry. Witness the resounding success of molecular biology, which unlocked the secrets of reproduction and inheritance under the noses of the classical biologists. So perhaps neurophysiology is really molecular biology? Some scientists studying the brain certainly think so. It is seriously, though in my view implausibly, suggested that DNA, which embodies the lessons of our evolution, is also the answer to the problems of memory, which nobody could deny is central to mental activity. What about psychology? There are, of course, old-fashioned psychologists who concern themselves with how human beings learn to speak or to adjust themselves to other people, but psychology is really neurophysiology; the most up-to-date psychologists need electrodes to stick into nerves and brains, knives for cutting bits out, and complicated electronic recording equipment for processing their measurements — though what the process of 'processing' is intended to achieve is not always made quite clear. And so on. Sociology is really psychology, economics is really sociology, history is really economics, and there the trail becomes indistinct.

I have been deliberately satirical in so describing the scientific reductionist, because his position only becomes clear when carried to its logical conclusion. But where is the fallacy? Because if we cannot find one, we must follow the argument where it seems to lead, into an intellectual wilderness populated by mad scientists trying to measure the positions and velocities of all the molecules within reach. Perhaps the best place to pick holes would be at a rather low level, with the assertion that chemistry is really physics, and see what this assertion amounts to. Roughly speaking, chemistry is concerned with the properties of matter under rather special conditions, such as those which prevail on earth. Under these conditions we can recognise distinct chemical substances, and the business of the chemist is to reveal the internal structure of these substances, and to account for their properties, including the ways in which they react with one another. The identity of a substance depends on the manner in which its constituent atoms are joined together. Usually, but not always, the atoms are bound together into identical clusters called molecules, so that the study of molecules is the major part of chemistry. But molecules come in all shapes and sizes, and must be brought to order before the chemist can state any significant generalisations about their behaviour. It is important to realise that

18

no-one except a chemist is competent to do this; certainly not a physicist, if only because physicists are so contemptuous of chemical distinctions – of 'stamp-collecting' in Rutherford's words. Let me take an actual example. In recent years there has been much interest among chemists in what are now called electrocyclic reactions. I imagine that only a handful of people in this room will have the slightest idea what electrocyclic reactions are, and I have no intention of trespassing on the ignorance of those who do not. Along comes a physicist, expert in quantum mechanics, which, he maintains, explains all chemistry in principle, and we ask him for an explanation of electrocyclic reactions. Does he offer one? No. His first words are 'What *are* electro-cyclic reactions?'. In order to answer his question we shall have to introduce him to chemical concepts which are not part of his intellectual armoury, and even then he may not understand why we asked the question. Actually to answer it he has to become, for the moment at least, a chemist. Only by so doing can he see what principles of physics may be relevant to its answer. Insofar as physics is what physicists do when they are left to get on with their own work, chemistry is not part of physics in any important sense. It has its own concepts and its own problems, the concepts being those which are relevant to the problems. This, of course, is not to deny that physical principles can be brought to bear on chemical phenomena, but the questions must be asked at the higher level before they can be examined at the lower.

But this is not the whole story; if it were, my objections to the reductionist position might seem tiresomely pedantic to, let us say, a molecular biologist engaged in the crystallographic study of virus particles. There is an even more cogent objection to the view that all higher level concepts must derive in the last resort from concepts in physics. Let me give a historical example. After Newton and Laplace it seemed that the secret of the universe was to be found in the laws of mechanics. These laws were thought to be deterministic in the sense that, given the states of motion of all material particles at one time, they would prescribe the states of motion of all the particles at any later time. But in the nineteenth century, before there had been any hint of indeterminacy in mechanics, a quite independent set of physical concepts emerged. Certain phenomena, such as the passage of heat from a hot body to a cold one, proved impossible to describe in purely mechanical terms. They called for the new concepts of temperature and entropy which, like the idea of disorder, only make sense when applied to physical systems in which the states of motion of the constituent particles are largely unknown. Statistical Mechanics, as the new subject was called, could obviously not be founded on mechanical principles alone, because heat and temperature were not mechanical but statistical concepts. There was nothing in mechanics itself to stop hot bodies from getting hotter, or cold bodies from growing colder. This in spite of the unquestioned authority of mechanics, when applied to systems in which the initial state was specified in every detail. So if, even within physics, one set of concepts are not reducible to another, what grounds can there be for asserting that the concepts and laws of any other science must be reducible to those of physics?

It will, perhaps, be as well if I try and summarise this critique of scientific reductionism before launching into our main topic, the nature of mind. It's all very well to say that one science rests upon another, if all we mean is that the laws of the former do not actually conflict with those of the latter. But this demand does not entail that the concepts of the higher science can necessarily be explicated in terms of the concepts of the lower science. Nor does it even imply that the laws of the higher science follow from those of the lower: this is clear from the universally conceded fact that thermo-dynamics does not follow logically from dynamics. Dynamics is quite indifferent to the arrow of time, and thermodynamics emphatically is not. Most thoughtful biologists implicitly accept this thesis. In his recent admirable book, *Le hasard et la necessité*, Jacques Monod is at pains to lay bare the distin-guishing features of living systems, or perhaps one should say, of life, in relation to the non-living world. He reinterprets the Darwinian thesis in modern terms, and shows how at every level, from the molecular to the visible, the evolution of life can be seen as the selection of what he calls 'teleonomic' variations, and their preservation by the fidelity of the hereditary process. This, if I may call it the *First Law of Biology*, is in style and conception totally unlike a law of physics, or even of chemistry, as I am sure Waddington would agree. But there are other scientists who remain unconvinced.

I recently attended a series of scientific meetings near Paris, at which a number of distinguished physicists and biologists were discussing the implications of theoretical physics for biology. It was a strange, indeed an unnerving, experience. In the politest possible way, some of the theoretical physicists seemed to be suggesting that if only the biologists would open their minds to certain theoretical possibilities which had been revealed by quantum mechanics, many of the more puzzling properties of living cells, and even of the brain, might become clear to them. The biologists, almost to a man, reacted to this advice with less than gratitude, and it was easy to see why. Indeed, at one point in the proceedings I could not help recalling the story of an Edwardian lady who found herself seated next to a stranger at dinner, and asked him about his work. 'Madam', he replied, 'I am a student of physics'. 'Oh really', she said, 'my husband always says that anyone with a classical education could get up physics in a fortnight'. But I must not give the impression that the scientific battle of the mind is being waged in the field of theoretical physics. To suggest that it was would be to incur the justified indignation of those scientists who actually study animals and their brains and their overt behaviour. An architect might well take offence if a town planner exchanged ideas over his head with a bricklayer, even though towns are ultimately built of bricks. So let us leave physics to the physicists, and see what the psychologists and neurophysiologists might be able to tell us about the nature of mind.

Psychology is still a young subject, struggling to be recognised as a science. I am not competent to review its history, but I suspect that it might make a rewarding Ph.D study in the sociology of science. The enormous success of the physical sciences in the nineteenth and early twentieth centuries called for some explanation, and generated a theory of science which laid great emphasis on quantitative measurement. Not surprisingly, this theory suited physics and chemistry very well, having been inspired by their example, but on the biological sciences its influence was perhaps a mixed blessing. It put pressure on the biologist to make his observations quantitative where possible, or at least to submit them to statistical analysis, but, as a consequence, it undervalued descriptive or taxonomic observations, and concepts which could not be worked into a quantitative mathematical theory. Little wonder, then, that psychology should suffer a severe attack of cold feet, and disown one of its great men, Sigmund Freud, in favour of white-coated experimenters on the learning abilities of rats and pigeons. Not that Freud was above criticism for his lack of statistical rigour; but how could anyone conduct an honest statistical analysis of material as complex and diverse as human dreams, for example? Nor would I suggest that nothing of value can be learned from carefully controlled experiments on animal and human behaviour; but what sort of information do such experiments yield, and can it possibly be used to illuminate our understanding of thought, as opposed to physical activity?

The behaviourist approach to psychology, as I interpret it, is founded on the determination to do away with human testimony as essentially unreliable and incapable of quantification. People's reaction times and pulse rates can be objectively measured, but their opinions and their interpretations of their experiences, though they may be noted by the experimenter, do not count as scientific evidence. In effect, the behaviourist treats the subject as a black box, which he subjects to measurable stimuli of various kinds, and which emits measurable responses. He attempts to establish a functional relationship between the two, in whatever terms suggest themselves to him. Needless to say, this is very difficult, and there is a quite

21

irresistible temptation to cheat. One way of cheating is to ask the subject why he responded as he did, but this would really give the game away. To prevent this kind of cheating, it is therefore recommended that all behavioural experiments should be conducted on dumb animals, but this does not prevent the experimenter from trying to interpret their behaviour by analogy with his own. The other way of cheating is, of course, to prise open the box and look inside. There must be some causal connection, surely, between the input stimulus and the output response; let us see if we can't trace the nervous pathways which lead from one to the other. At this point, of course, the behaviourist has turned into a neurophysiologist, so let us see what the professional neuro-physiologist has to tell us.

To the neurophysiologist, the word 'mind' is even more suspect than to the experimental psychologist. His intellectual orientation is set by the word 'neuron', and anything which isn't neuronal isn't neurophysiology. The mind, whatever it is, certainly isn't composed of neurons, but the brain is. So let us put behind us the outworn concept of mind, and try to understand how the brain works. It may take many years, or even decades, but patience and experimental skill will eventually be rewarded. We already know quite a bit about axons, dendrites, synapses, and what have you; ultimately we may hope to have a more or less complete map of the central nervous sytem and we shall be home. This little caricature of the neurophysiologist is, I admit, quite unfair to those devoted scientists who have told us what we know about the structure of the most complex system in the universe, and it does very much less than justice to those who feel that we have a long way to go before we shall be able to understand even the main principles on which the brain works. But, loyalty to one's colleagues apart, I suspect that neurophysiology alone can never lead to a full understanding of the brain. The real difficulty, as I see it, is in defining the problem. It is all very well to ask for a neuro-physiological interpretation of the physical activity of an animal, but how can the neurophysiolo-gist provide us with an interpretation of its mental activity, unless we can find an independent way of describing mental activity? It's no good defining mental activity in neurophysio-logical terms, because this would preclude explaining it in those terms. In short, if we want the neurophysiologist to help us to understand how the brain works, we must tell him, in non-physiological terms, what we mean by the word 'works'. And at this point we find ourselves on the frontiers of thought.

Again it will be as well if I summarise before continuing. In the last few decades — though this trend is less evident now — psychologists have tended to play down the signifi-cance of subjective evidence and to concentrate on those things that can be measured with clocks, electrodes, and chemical tests. But the baby is in danger of being thrown away with the bath water. We might, it is true, be able to control rats, pigeons, and other pests, by feeding them with brain hormones, or otherwise manipulating their stimulus-response patterns; but when it comes to human beings surely the only ultimate justification for a scientific study of the mind is to enable us to understand ourselves better, and if possible to improve our mental capacities. How can we possibly do this, if we turn our backs on thought itself, and consider only its physical manifestations? Surely it is time that we admitted mental concepts into the scientific study of the mind; but what is a mental concept?

At this point I leave the conventional sciences for a while to consider what other attempts have been made to elucidate the nature of thought. As usual, we find that many of the best ideas have a very long history. One of the oldest intellectual disciplines is Logic — as Kenny said yesterday — the study of the validity of inferences. If there are any concepts which must find a place in a theory of the mind, then inference is surely among them, and logic used to be regarded as embodying the laws of thought. The phrase 'the laws of thought' sounds strange to the modern ear at a time when scientific laws are taken to be business-like statements about down-to-earth matters like magnetism, or crystals, or cell membranes; and logic has come a long way since Aristotle. In a modern textbook of logic one is rather unlikely to discover any reference to the way our minds work. Certainly none of the arguments will appeal in any way to facts about human intelligence. The only symptom of concern with human thought is an occasional appeal to the reader's intuition as to how the symbolism may be informally interpreted, and perhaps a few examples for him to work out. If the author offers any apology for his subject this is much more likely to refer to the foundations of mathematics than to human reasoning *per se*. All this is entirely healthy, so long as the ultimate goal of the enterprise is not overlooked. If logic is to be justified solely as a critique of mathematical reasoning, then what is the justification for mathematics itself, or rather, what *is* mathematics? To ask this question is to invite the sarcastic reply that mathematics is what mathematicians do, either for their own benefit, if they are pure, or for the benefit of others, if they are applied. But even this riposte leaves open the question: how are we to decide whether a particular piece of mathematics is right or wrong? And here an appeal to some independent court is unavoidable. In the last resort, a piece of mathematics must stand or fall by whether it meets the demands of human reason; and we are back in the realm of the mind. In any but the most formalistic age, it would seem entirely natural to suggest that our mathematics is inspired by the attempt to capture the essence of our own processes of reasoning.

Another idea of great antiquity, referred to yesterday by Kenny, is that the secret of human thought is to be found in the study of human language. Language may not be the only medium in which thoughts can be expressed, but it is the faculty which most obviously distinguishes us from other animals, and permits the philosopher to discuss, the scientist to describe, not only the world but the nature of man. As most members of this audience are undoubtedly aware, the study of language has suddenly entered a new age. The leader of the new linguistics was, of course, the American linguist, Noam Chomsky. Chomsky's special contribution to linguistic thought was his comparison between the grammatical sentences of a natural language and the theorems of a logical system. Modern logic is conducted in symbols, as language is conducted in words, and there are strict rules in logic for determining whether a string of symbols represents a theorem; that is, whether it can be derived from a particular set of strings called the axioms. To say this might give the impression that Chomsky's primary concern was with form rather than with content, and this impression would not be entirely misleading. But to Chomsky and his school the concept of form gives place to that of structure, and the structure of a sentence in a natural language is identified with the manner in which that sentence is derived from the vocabulary of the language by the application of grammatical rules. I shall not go into detail now, as we shall be discussing language very fully in later sessions. I merely want to emphasise that language is an exceedingly rich mine of information about our mental processes, that its description is a highly non-trivial undertaking, which has already led to some general insights which are far from obvious, and that the study of language is no less scientific an enterprise than the study of aggressive behaviour or of courtship patterns, as its primary data is equally open to observation and to theoretical interpretation. As in other branches of science, a particular observation, or its interpretation, must always be open to revision, but the categories within which ideas about language must be framed seem to be much more nearly in keeping with a science of the mind than those which must be used for interpreting, let us say, the blink reflex, or the effects of narcotics upon attention.

So logic and linguistics seem to be directly concerned with the nature of mental processes in a way in which neurophysiology is not, and physics could not possibly ever be. But how are they to be integrated into psychology, or at least into that part of psychology which has survived the ravages of behaviourism? Because the picture is not as black as I painted it; there are many psychologists who pay their subjects the compliment of attending to their reports, and are prepared to incorporate into their theories concepts such as recognition, or interpretation, or decision, which do not lend themselves readily to statistical analysis. I want to suggest that the problem of describing the mind becomes very much clearer if we recognise that in speaking of 'the mind' we are not speaking of a static or passive entity, but of an enormously complex pattern of processes, far too rapid for us to reflect upon as we carry them out. One of the most interesting psychological case-studies on record is that of the late Professor A. C. Aitken, of this university. Aitken was probably the most prodigious mental calculator in all history, as well as being a first class mathematician. He was able to recount, in moderate detail, what happened in his mind when he was asked, for example, to work out the cube root of a nine-figure number; and his reports, which it would be perverse to disregard, reveal an ability to run through an incredibly complex set of mental processes in far less time than it took him to report them. He lived long enough to witness the marvels of modern computing, and it is said that he regarded the computer as an unfair competitor. And this brings me to my last point.

The computer is, without doubt, the most interesting of modern inventions. Many people see it as a threat, of course, but the threat arises from its ability to do what no machine has ever done before: to carry out logical operations. It is interesting to think what a neurophysiologist or a physicist might make of a computer, if they had never set eyes on one before. The physicist would discover inside it a large number of magnetic memory elements, and there his interest would probably stop. The neuro-physiologist would trace the wires leading in and out of the memory, and make an anatomical map, including the various pieces of peripheral equipment; he might also note that sharp pulses travelled hither and thither, and activated the peripherals in an irregular way. But neither of them would really understand what was happening unless someone came along and explained about programs, and about computing languages, in which programs are written. The analogy with human thinking begins to fail at this point, because human beings can of course think very well without being programmed; perhaps I shouldn't say without ever having been programmed, but without being programmed at the time they do the thinking. But it does bring out one point of substance for our discussions, namely that the whole enterprise of understanding our minds is doomed to failure unless someone – and it had better be the psychologist – is prepared to undertake the description of mental processes in terms at least as abstract as those which are needed for describing computing 'software', as it is called. It is a commonplace to say that computing is the implementation of lógical algorithms, that is, precisely ordered sets of logical instructions. Isn't it about time that psychology embraced the idea of an algorithm, and began to formulate a theory of thought in algorithmic terms? The only risk I can see in adopting this strategy is that it might fail to throw any light on the nature of thought − which I very much doubt − or that it might fail to illuminate all our problems − which seems very likely but can hardly count as an argument against making the attempt.

In this talk I have probably done very much less than was expected of me. I have not attempted to analyse the essential nature of mind, or to list all those mental faculties which we hold most precious. Others are better qualified than I to do that. All I have tried to do is to show that neither neurophysiology nor behaviourist psychology will suffice for the construction of a science of the mind, because their concepts are not mental but physical. The initiative must come from a more abstract level of description, such as logic or linguistics, and a psychological theory worthy of the name must accommodate the concepts of these subjects. It goes without saying that the psychology of the future must harmonise with the findings of neurophysiology, just as chemistry must harmonise with physics; but neither physics nor physiology can possibly dictate the laws which describe how our minds work.

Discussion

KENNY

I've been asked to start the discussion, but perhaps I'm not a very good person to start, because I am in sympathy with ninety-five percent of what Longuet-Higgins said. In the first part of his paper he argued in a general way against the programme of reductionism in science, and with that I'm in entire agreement. In the second part of his paper, he argued more in particular that he thought that the science of the mind, which is, as yet, something rather in the future, could not be reduced to either of the existing sciences of behavioural psychology or of neuro-physiology. And here there were two points with which I disagree. Professor Longuet-Higgins admitted that his account of the neuro-physiologist was something of a caricature. Though he didn't say so, I think that perhaps his account of the behaviourist was also something of a caricature, and, having myself last night been critical of behaviourism, I'd like to defend the behaviourist in one respect.

I think that behaviourism was characterised by Longuet-Higgins as an approach determined to do away with human testimony in investigating its subject matter. I think that he is wrong and that behaviourists are right, in saying that one shouldn't pay much attention to people's testimony about their thoughts, if by testimony we mean the kind of thing which Longuet-Higgins seems to mean − the remarks made, say, by the late Professor Aitken, about what went on in his mind when he did his prodigious calculation, or for that matter, the kind of thing which Waddington quoted last night from Einstein. What makes the thoughts of Einstein great − indeed, what makes them thoughts at all − is not what imagery or what visceral thrills he said occurred while he was thinking out the answer to his problems; it's rather that the answers, when he comes to express them in symbols, whether in mathematical symbols or in language, can be understood by others, can be criticised by others, can be used by others to guide and inform their own researches and their own experiments. If we are to study human intelligent thought, we mustn't take the expression of those thoughts as being mere causal results of the true hidden thought of which these are just the visible effects. The verbal expression of the thought is itself an instance, and indeed the paradigm instance, of the phenomenon which is to be studied. It's the preeminent instance of that phenomenon and it's the first thing that we have to study. To this extent the behaviourist, it seems to me, is perfectly right, though I'm not sure how far Longuet-Higgins would in the long run disagree, since later in his paper he said that language is a primary datum which is open to observation, and that I certainly agree with.

In the second place I want to take up a remark which is perhaps unfair to take up because it was meant at least partly as a joke. Longuet-Higgins said that the late Professor Aitken regarded the computer as an unfair competitor of the mathematician. Now, though this was a joke, I think that Longuet-Higgins does really believe that computers can do arithmetic. In one sense, of course, it is obviously true that computers can do arithmetic, and can do it better than we can. But computers can do arithmetic better than we can in precisely the same sense as clocks can tell the time better than we can; in the sense that, if you want to know what the time is, you do better to look at a clock than to introspect or to ask a neighbour who hasn't got a watch. But of course, in another sense, clocks can't tell the time at all: it is we who tell the time, using clocks as our instruments. Clocks can't tell the time, because clocks can't know the time, and if clocks could tell the time they wouldn't know what to do with it when they told it.

LONGUET-HIGGINS

Well, I should be ashamed to spoil that last point; let me take Kenny's earlier point. I think that Einstein's thoughts and Aitken's thoughts are interesting, and I think they are instructive and they tell us something about the way people think, or the way some people can think − and after all it's what the mind *can* do which is of more interest than what it always does. The highest manifestations obviously are exceedingly interesting, but if we didn't believe that it was of significance to tell other people what went through our minds when we solved problems, then what the hell is a university for? At a university we try to teach people how to think, and we do this by introspecting as best we can. There isn't very much theory about this yet, but we do describe to other people our own thought processes, hoping that the descriptions which we give them may appeal to them and may help them to direct their minds in a similar way. No, I just cannot allow that it's ultimately of no concern as to how Einstein solves his problems. If we could teach ourselves to think in the way that Einstein does, no doubt we'd think a great deal better.

Well now, the second point, arising out of that: I wasn't suggesting for a moment that one should disregard overt behaviour. I was merely suggesting that there are people who put blinkers on their scientific research. I wasn't criticising behaviour*al* psychology, let me say; I was talking about a certain philosophical school in psychology, called the behaviour*ists*. I don't suppose there are any behaviour*ists* in this room, although doubtless there are many behaviour*al* psychologists. But a behaviourist psychologist is a person who holds a certain dogma about psychology, and I couldn't find any other way in which to represent this dogma clearly, but to say that it excludes from serious consideration human testimony, so that we are only allowed to pay serious attention to the way that this thing responds when we do this and that to it. Of course, there are dangers in believing what people say, because people can be terribly misled about their own mental processes; but one doesn't want to disregard any clues which one might be able to use.

LUCAS

I am in an awkward position, because I agree with Longuet-Higgins' conclusions, which are admirable and true and worthy to be believed, but my logical conscience doesn't allow me to accept the arguments by which he reaches them. That is to say, it seems to me quite evident, if one looks at the whole field of human knowledge, that reductionism doesn't work and is untrue. What is difficult, though, is to see how the reductionist arguments may be met, and I don't think as yet that their case has been properly answered. Some points have been made, for instance the stamp-collecting argument is a very important one, and I go entirely along with that. Aristotle was the first to put this forward — he called them 'formal causes' — what sort of thing it is. And it's clearly of the greatest importance in chemistry, also in biology. Biologists have realised that it is so important that they have a special name for it: taxonomy, and if this isn't enough, we can consider the case of doctors where much the rarest skill and much the most important skill is that of diagnosis — 'what is it that is wrong with you?' Now this far I go, with Longuet-Higgins, in seeing that there is more than one question that we have to face, and it's because there is more than one question that not all the sciences are the same science. Biology asks different questions, and therefore can't be reduced to chemistry or physics. But the difficulty is to be sure that the different questions don't get in the way of each other. And now I'm just going to raise two difficulties, and try and give one answer which may not do.

One point which I think is worth making, and that we are, and rightly, worried about is this: when the biologist is asking a question we feel that what the chemist or the physicist has to say is going to be of very great importance; but then how come that it doesn't completely answer the question? For instance, one can't manage without air. It seems that if you know all about the oxygen supply surely you must know all about respiration. And in answer to this I want to put forward a slightly sophisticated logician's move, which is to talk about bound variables. The crucial point is that, whereas the Laplacean physicist thought that he would be able to know where every molecule of oxygen was, and every other molecule, and work out from an initial state description the whole of the subsequent course of the universe, the biologist doesn't need this information, and would find it entirely irrelevant, because from his point of view one molecule of oxygen is as good as another. And this indefinite replaceability is one of the ways by which we can distinguish what is true, in the reductionist's case, from what is false.

A second point, which I'm not so sure about, is to take the difficulty, which seems to arise as we think about the reductionist case, that if I know all about something very simple then I must be able to answer more complicated questions, because they must be definable in terms of necessary and sufficient conditions of the very simple. This is an old, old thesis, a thesis of logical atomism, and how this is to be answered I think can be partly seen by an analogy in the human disciplines, where we often have some rather general, vague concept — motive was suggested earlier — which clearly is connected with behaviour. I can't be really and truly generous if I don't ever give anybody anything, yet it's not to be defined in terms of behaviour; because I can be generous in this way or in that, or the other; my behaviour is evidence for my generosity or not, but it's always only *prima facie* evidence, which can be rebutted by further evidence of my failure to be generous on some other occasion. And what I want just simply to air for the moment is the possibility that we shall find part of the answer to the reductionist's case in moving from the logic of necessary and sufficient conditions to the logic which we are much more familiar with, in history, in the law court, in philosophy, of stating a case, facing objections to it, rebutting those objections, and then having those rebuttals again turned against ourselves.

WADDINGTON

Could I make a remark about reductionism, because I think I'm somewhat more sympathetic to it than Longuet-Higgins. I've always in the past really considered myself rather strongly anti-reductionist. It's only after listening to him that I am beginning to have some doubts as to whether I'm as anti as I once thought.

The real snag of reductionism, it seems to me, arises if you suppose that we really know all there is to be known about the physical entities and laws. Now I've lived long enough to have been taught chemistry at a time when what I was taught is now totally changed. I was taught that molecules were made up of groups of atoms which stick together with valancy bonds, like little hooks sticking out of them in certain directions, with which they could join together. This left absolutely no possibility of the very large scale protein molecules with their tertiary structure and allosteric behaviour and such things, which are now explained as depending on incomplete saturation of the bonds between the atoms that are primarily joined together in the basic molecule. That concept didn't occur forty years ago, at any rate in the chemistry I was taught; it's been added on since. You must, I think, always realise that we don't know all about the basic physical entities, we don't know all about the electron, we don't know all about the quantum. If we discover new phenomena, which can't be squeezed into what we already knew, we just add a bit to what we thought we knew about the original, elementary structures. At least, we can try to do that, but I don't think we always can do it. I am quite in agreement with Longuet-Higgins that mental phenomena have to be described in terms of mental systems, and the questions to ask about intentions and mental operations cannot be phrased into physical terms – or at least, they can't *as yet* be phrased into physical terms, in such a way that you could get an answer by any modification of basic physical concepts. Maybe we never will be able to. But I'm sympathetic enough to the reductionist position to say we should at least try to; that if we have complex mental phenomena, and have to describe them in a non-physical way, we will want to ask non-physical questions about them, but we can try to invent new physical explanations.

In biology, for instance, it might be said that to all the questions we want to ask about evolution we give an answer in terms of phenomena such as natural selection, which you can hardly translate into physical terms, or if you did it would be so fantastically clumsy as to be unusable. You may have to apply different types of explanation to answer the questions you want to ask. But unless you try to get your answers in terms congruent with the other sciences as you know them already, you are liable to go off and invent specific explanations which you will never be able to incorporate into the rest of science. In the specific case of neurophysiology, have the physical factors told us anything relevant to mental events? The sort of questions one wants to ask about linguistics, or about logic, are questions that have to be framed in terms of things like algorithmic programmes, or in some sort of mentalistic terms, and cannot be framed easily in terms of the passage of currents among neurons. On the other hand, the fact that we know that when events are going on in the brain they take the form of electric currents passing through many cells in many different regions of the brain, does give us some indication of the kind of animal we are dealing with; the kind of thing we are talking about. For instance, there are plenty of cells in the brain; many more single cells than are needed to provide one cell per word in the dictionary. I'm not certain whether there are enough to provide one cell for each sentence anybody says in his lifetime, but I shouldn't be terribly surprised. So you could have imagined that mental events involve single specific individual cells, or a smallish number of individual cells for each mental event. This would have meant that a mental event had quite a different basic character from that which it has when it involves a few millions of cells, reverberating and interacting, with currents passing between them. It does seem to me that although the neuro-physiological understanding is not yet refined enough to shed any bright light on mental concepts, it nevertheless does give us an indication of the kind of thing we are talking about when we speak about a logical algorithm.

LONGUET-HIGGINS

I don't think I can really deal with John Lucas' point in a moment, but I think I might be able to say something in reply to Waddington. I think there is quite a difference between the reductionist position as it might have been before 1927 and the position as it is now, because — though it sounds terribly dogmatic to say so — we really do know that chemical phenomena are determined by the Schrodinger equation. The equation has survived a fantastic amount of testing, and it really seems to be right. So it's no good trying to fiddle with the foundations. As for the other point which you made — if you want to understand the tertiary structure of proteins, well, if you've got a relevant chemical concept *that* might need revision, indeed it might; which just goes to show how chemical concepts are not the same thing as physical concepts.

Just to make a remark about the brain, and all those neurons and so forth, I think the computer is particularly helpful here, helping one to think clearly about the relation between different kinds of problem. If I have a computing language, and a program, and a computer, I can ask different kinds of question about a computation. We can ask what's the logic of the computation, or we can ask, how does the computer interpret the language. Finally we can ask how does the computer actually work — has it got solid state circuits and so forth. If I advance a theory about the way this computation is implemented, which simply doesn't fit with the actual physical structure of the computer, of course I'm talking rubbish. And it's that sense in which we can say that the higher level — more abstract — concepts or assertions have got to square with the assertions at the lower level. It's very difficult to make a general statement making it clear quite how the higher level generalisations relate to the lower level restrictions, but I think this is a case in which we can see very clearly in what manner that relation is to be considered.

Third Lecture. Determinism and Life

As I said at our first meeting, I am a biologist, really an experimental biologist; I'm not a philosopher and I have little experience of dealing with the mind. Therefore this lecture will be rather a biologist's down-to-earth lecture, before we go back to more refined philosophical considerations of the body.

I want to ask whether questions we normally ask about the mind, free-will, determinism and so on, are really phrased in terms of an adequate *model*. I'm going to suggest that they very often are not; that very often people think that we are dealing with a system in which the details of the output correspond precisely to the details of the input; and I'm going to say that that is not the way many biological things work, and I don't think the mind does so either. And then, many of the questions about free-will — can you make up your mind to do something — are usually discussed as though you were a man in a padded cell, totally isolated; and of course most people, most of the time at least, are not in padded cells, but are in situations in which they are continually showered with all sorts of inputs from their environment. And in particular from other people.

I shall approach by asking what we know of the character of other biological systems, simpler than a mind.

This can be 'accused' of being a sort of 'reductionism'. I agree, but I think it legitimate, so long as we recognise that appeal to ('reduction to') a lower level entity should never be allowed to force us to reject anything discernible in the higher entity. What we may have to do is to change our concept of the lower entity to accommodate the new properties we find that it can, under some circumstances, exhibit. When I said this, the other night, using an example from chemistry, Christopher Longuet-Higgins rebuked me, saying that the Schrodinger equations contain everything that there is to know about the interactions between atoms and molecules. Conceivably; but are they not a trifle on the inscrutable side? No one can solve them for anything more complex than the hydrogen atom, and, if they do contain everything necessary to understand protein molecules, no one can get it out of them. So when, some time ago, Jacob and Monod in Paris discovered that protein molecules, highly complex molecules, could exhibit a property called allostery, they got the Nobel Prize for it. Allostery is a name I don't suppose many of you have heard before. It's the phenomon that if you act on one sensitive site in a complex body, sometimes another sensitive site somewhere else gets ready to be active or becomes active; a phenomenon, one might, say, that is not outside the ordinary run of sexual experiences. But it was quite novel about protein molecules, and its discovery there did, and quite justly, obtain the Nobel Prize. So I think that reductionism — attempting to reduce things to the simpler elements — may be OK if you do it carefully enough. I'm going to suggest that many of the discussions one reads about the mind and about determinism don't do it carefully enough, and actually reduce too far, to things like Newtonian billiard ball atoms, when they ought to have stopped at some intermediate stage.

So, let's consider some of these intermediate stages. One of the main characteristics of biological systems is a sort of inherent cussedness. When I was at school we learnt something called La Chatelier's rule, which was about the world in general, to the effect that if you do anything to something, it will react in such a way as to cancel out what you've done. It's not actually absolutely true, I think, but it's a fairly widely experienced situation, and it certainly applies very well to many biological systems. If you run very fast and increase the CO_2 content of your blood, the body does something that reduces the CO_2 and brings it back to normal. Similarly if you change the pH of your blood, its acidity, again there's a very efficient mechanism for restoring it to normality. This is a tendency to restore the status quo. It's usually called 'homeostasis', keeping the thing stationary, at the same situation. A more general phenomenon is one where the things are changing all the time. Being in my professional experience an embryologist and evolutionist, I'm always used to things that change, and don't stay still. Embryos never stay still, they go on developing. But they go on developing along definite pathways, and if you chop a bit out, or add a bit on, or do something like that to an embryo, unless you go too far, it usually succeeds in getting itself back to normality and producing the normal end result. This is not a stabilised situation; it's a stabilised pathway of change; what I call 'homeorhesis'.

To take a very simple example of this sort of phenomenon; if you drop the soap in the bath, and pull the plug, the soap goes down the drain, pretty well independently of where you dropped it. This is, of course, due to there being a physical constraint on the system, the bath with the drain at its lowest point.

In biological systems, there is not, in general, anything which can be compared to the bath. The constraints on the system have to be generated by the system itself. This requires, firstly, that the system must be complex, containing many component processes; and secondly, that these must interact in ways which 'stabilise' (better, 'canalise') a certain pathway of change, by feedback devices which monitor whether one

34

component is going too far off track, and if so operate to bring it back. Such a pathway of change is a 'chreod'. In a chreodic system, so long as external factors do not push the system beyond certain limits, the end result is independent of what the inputs precisely are – the system will finish up at its inbuilt end-point, just as any stream within a certain valley will finish up flowing out by the main river. Unless, of course, it is pushed across a watershed, when it will flow down another valley into another river.

Many biological systems, for instance embryos, have a character which cannot be described by a single chreod, but only by an 'epigenetic landscape', containing many chreods separated by 'watersheds' (which technically have the perhaps unfortunate name of 'catastrophe regions'). For instance there are 'watersheds' separating developmental pathways leading from the early embryonic condition to adult nerve, muscle, epidermis, various glands etc.

The mind has to be regarded as a system of chreodic systems. Each of its components is complex, with many sub-components, and these interact in ways which tend to stabilise the patterns of activity. Let me give some examples:

First, biochemical. We know at least a score of abnormal genes in man, which cause the appearance of abnormal enzymes, which in turn bring about abnormalities in mental functioning and thus in behaviour. The normal forms of all these enzymes must be involved in normal brain functioning.

Next anatomical. The actual course of the nerves, and their interconnections, is best known for one of the evolutionarily oldest and most primitive parts of the brain, the cerebellum, which is concerned with learning and then controlling (unconsciously) skilled movements, such as running downstairs. Even though our knowledge of the 'wiring' of the cerebellum is probably only roughly accurate, it is certain that many of the cells function by monitoring the activity of other cells, and signalling the result on to still another group, so as to adjust their activity accordingly. That is to say, many of the cells are acting as feedbacks, to keep the whole activity within certain limits.

Then language. A word (or concept) is a chreod covering a certain range of values. (An orange may be a tangerine, a mandarin, a Navel, a Seville etc.)

Finally, consider computer intelligence. People who are trying to program computers to carry out mindlike activities have had to build chreodic properties into them, that is, the ability to deal with individual details in connection with larger systems. When Winograd was constructing a program to allow a computer to understand normal language, he had to ensure that when presented with the input 'Is there a block on a green table? What colour is it?' the last word, 'it', was not taken alone, but in its place in the whole context, which makes it clear that the question is about the colour of the block, not of the table. Unless such comparisons can be made between different parts of an utterance, and a balance struck between them, natural language would not remain within the chreod of 'making sense', but would seem chaotic and impossible to interpret.

The paradox of the mind is that although it is the most flexible instrument which has been produced by evolution, making an enormous range of reactions, each very appropriate to a larger variety of inputs than any other system can take cognisance of, it does this, not by letting 'specifically complex input' be translated directly into a correspondingly specific output, but by inserting an intermediate stage, in which the 'demands' of the input are matched by a suitable combination of pre-existing lower-level (less complex) multi-purpose chreods (programmes, symbols). For instance, we usually formulate a new thought by a new combination of existing words, rather than by just defining a new word.

Now any system which has a chreodic character, that is, a tendency to change in some definite direction, or to reach some definite end-point, could be said to exhibit an unconscious will, with the end-point as its goal. Thus I am claiming that all mental events have something of a will-like character.

Of course, in pre-Freudian days, will was nearly always taken to mean conscious will — except by a very few sophisticated novelists, such as Lady Murasaki in 10th century Japan. Even now, the problem which troubles most people is the effectiveness or otherwise of conscious free will. What, if anything, does the concept of chreods allow us to say about it? Consciousness undoubtedly has a largely private character, and is therefore difficult for science to get to grips with. (Kenny will probably discuss further just how private it is). I can only offer some rather disconnected remarks.

First, (a parenthesis), I would like to ask whether consciousness is so very important after all. Some Eastern religions have attributed the highest values to meditation, not action; for them free will, or even consciousness of the external world in general, are not so very important. Even if we place greater value on Good Action, rather than Good Being, might it not be argued that the really Good Man just acts rightly as a straightforward expression of what he is, without having to think consciously, or argue with himself, about it? Is our emphasis on the problem of free will part of the Western World's insistence — still further emphasised in the Puritan tradition — that no action can be of value unless it is difficult and unpleasant?

It has not been too difficult to discover something about the machinery which decides whether conscious experience will occur or not. We know about brain centres which control sleep, or arousal, or even rather more specific experiences of pleasure, discomfort and so on.

This is far from telling us exactly what we shall be conscious of. We clearly are never conscious of everything which is available for us to be conscious of at any moment. We tend to be conscious, firstly, of anything unexpected — if any of the audience had a bright blue face, I should probably consciously notice it, even in a general glance round. Secondly, we tend to be conscious of anything relevant to some contest to which we are directing attention. This 'direction of attention' is something much more specific than mere general arousal — I think it is one of the main mysteries in the operations of the mind. It seems to me that the important questions about Free Will are closely allied to the problem of how we can direct or concentrate attention on some particular context.

In the first place, I want to make the point that the subjective feeling of free will is not at all connected with the logical problem with which it is usually associated in discussion, namely whether we are dealing with a system which is not subject to the deterministic laws of causation. It is only in the most trivial instances, when we are least conscious of 'making a choice' — for instance when we have to pick up either a cup of tea or of coffee while engaged in a conversation about something much more interesting — that we can be satisfied to ask whether our action is determined by cause and effect or whether there is some Stochastic Demon throwing dice inside us. In more important choices — shall I get married to Joan and start earning a salary, or stay on as a student and get Honours? — the feeling is not just of the operations of Chance — though that may also be involved — but rather of being pulled in several directions.

One can describe the situation by saying that the state of one's mental apparatus is such that it is poised on a watershed between two or more chreods. It is in a 'catastrophe region'; and a slight diversion one way or the other will take it into one or another valley of the epigenetic landscape, which may lead to very different end-results. Perhaps we are particularly likely to be conscious of the existence of choices between chreods when we are posed on the watersheds between them.

One might take the view that the feeling of 'exerting will power' is merely a symptom which arises when our internal state is somewhere in the watershed or catastrophe region; that the strength of the feeling, or the demands on our will, simply reflect the strength of the opposing forces which are tending to push us in one or other direction; but that the outcome of the opposition of these forces is fully determined in advance, and that however much we feel we are exerting will power, we are not influencing the situation at all, merely registering it by a certain emotional response. I think the gist of the debate about free will is to decide whether this is an adequate description.

In the first place, I should argue that it is certainly inadequate to suggest that the outcome of a conflict between two or more internal drives which we have at any given moment is determined by the strengths which those drives have built up over any substantial period. To suppose so leaves out of account that we normally live in surroundings which continually bombard us with unforeseeable inputs — and the chreods between which we are poised are systems which 'canalise', towards distant goals, not only the internal forces which arise within us from our genetic endowment and our previous experience, but also the immediate input with which we are showered by our environment. And our environment usually includes other persons, and we cannot tell in advance just which ones we will run into and what they will communicate to us, thus contributing a push off the crest of the watershed in one or other direction. This liability to unforeseeable inputs gives our actions some degree of the 'indeterminateness' or rather unpredictability of the classical example of 'chance operations', the tossing of a coin. No one supposes that, when you toss a penny, the deterministic laws of classical physics are in any way violated — but the inputs into the systems of movements are so many that the outcome cannot be predicted.

My own strongest experiences of free will — or the exertion of will power — have probably been in the last stages of quarter mile and half mile races. When you are within fifty yards of the tape, you feel: just how far can you concentrate on putting on a sprint at the expense of pushing your oxygen debt, and the lactic acid of your blood, to levels which feel most unpleasant? The point I made above is that some unforeseeable input from the external world can make a real difference. The stop watch will show that you did better when out of the corner of your eye you saw some other man's beastly legs pounding away just half a yard ahead of you, than when you didn't. And you felt you 'tried' harder: was this just a reflection of what the visual evidence of his presence deterministically did to you, or did it make any difference?

Well, the evidence that he was there, and winning, only spurred you on to cliff-hang a bit more perilously on the 'run' side of the watershed because you went on *concentrating attention* on a particular objective, winning the race. But supposing you had diverted your attention to something else. All sorts of odd things happen at the extremes of physical endurance — you may feel you are really three feet up in the air above your head, watching; you may feel, you have got your nostrils and mouth fully open to take in the air you need, but there is no muscle power to suck it in, it is all being used in your legs. If you did divert attention to consciously experiencing these things, you wouldn't run faster. But *could* you control your attention in this way?

This sort of question – and not any professional expertise about Heisenberg and quantum indeterminacy – is, in my opinion, the crucial issue about the effectiveness of willing.

I will put the question in more general terms:

(i) the effectiveness of an external or internal input, in influencing the output from the brain, is, usually at least, greater when that input is consciously experienced than when it is not;

(ii) it is more likely to be consciously experienced when 'attention' is directed towards some context with which it is connected;

(iii) if, therefore, we can 'will' to concentrate attention on some particular context, we could control the effectiveness of the various inputs impinging on our mental activities at that moment.

Can we?

I do not think the question is answerable in terms of existing science. The problem is one of the content of consciousness. You – or those of you who have not got bored – are conscious of my voice and what I am saying; but there are many other things you might be conscious of; you are unlucky if there is not a pretty girl, or a handsome boy, within a few yards, and you might be concentrating your attention on them. What directs your attention? That is the question. But how could science approach it? There is nothing in fundamental physics – the inscrutable Schrodinger equations – which opens even a possibility that a system of atoms might not merely react to its surroundings but consciously *experience* them. Nothing even in such more complex scientific entities as genes, or cells, opens any door out of the realm of 'input stimuli and output reactions', into the realm of conscious experience. Until we have something to say about what it is which differentiates a conscious experience from an unconscious reaction to a stimulus, we cannot throw any light on the basic question – what decides, and how, which of our mental and perceptual activities is enabled to 'register' as 'information' which plays its part in the deciding whether we slip off the watershed down into one chreodic valley or the other? But one thing is, I think, clear. In discussing free will, we are not inhabiting a world to which Newtonian or Laplacian determinism, or Quantum Indeterminacy, have any relevance. We are concerned with a chreodic world, in which outputs are largely independent of inputs; and we are asking questions about the distribution of something – Conscious Attention – which we can experience but cannot describe.

Discussion

LUCAS

Waddington was rather defensive at the outset – he feared that he might be charged with reductionism but I thought the charge which was much more likely to be levelled against him was that of vitalism. The chreods are strongly reminiscent of the entelechies (another Greek word used in the last century by biologists) which were found by many biologists to be necessary and by many other scientists to be impossible, as a means of describing the phenomena of the organic living world. What I would like to extract from this part of Waddington's lecture as part of a programme for the whole of this course of lectures is to try and see what is true about vitalism and how this can be reconciled with what is true in mechanism — as it were, how the controversies of the last century can now be resolved at a higher plane. We know in part that the homeostatic mechanisms which the cyberneticians have invented and which we are fairly familiar with enable us to go some of the way, but it is fairly evident that Waddington does not want to say that his chreods are merely homeostats, otherwise he wouldn't have introduced a new word. For myself, I recognise some of what he is trying to put forward (although I am unhappy about some of the examples — the oranges, the seville oranges and mandarins — this did not seem to be a very happy chreod, but no doubt Waddington will be able to explain it rather more fully). More generally what I think we have to recognise is that some sort of teleological explanation, explanations in terms of purposes (we ask 'What is that organ for?', we ask of certain patterns of animal behaviour 'Why is the robin billing and cooing?') is essential if we are to get an adequate understanding of biological phenomena and, *a fortiori*, of specifically human affairs. But we have to raise a sort of neo-Kantian question 'How are teleological explanations possible?' That is to say, 'How are they compatible with the kind of explanation which Longuet-Higgins is always going to trot out his Schrodinger equations to prove as being absolutely basic and essential?' And this is a question which we have not yet begun to answer.

I now want to turn to the latter part of Waddington's lecture where he was talking about freewill and consciousness, and where he was putting forward the suggestion that consciousness was perhaps dispensable from an elucidation of the problem of freewill, although noticeably not dispensable from his account of the universe as a whole, and I think we should be prepared to go quite a long way with Waddington. That is to say, what is crucial to whether a person is responsible for his actions or not, is not that he is very conscious of acting rightly: we are right to be rather suspicious of people who judge the moral worth of their actions from how hard they can persuade themselves that they at that time were resisting the temptations which beset them. Rather we should be prepared to count to a man's credit the unremembered acts that constitute the greater part of a good man's life and seize as the crucial way into the concept of responsibility that which the word evidently originally meant — '*respondeo*; I answer' — answerability to the question 'why did you do this?' The person needn't at the time be answering the question; it is only the sort of answer he would have given. This goes right back to the Greeks — Socrates was very keen on 'logon echein te kai didonai': 'to have and to be able to give reasons for what you are doing', and the question which we need to consider is whether there is a place in our account of the mind, and possibly in our account of other phenomena, for this question or whether it is, as has often been suggested and as mechanism seems to suggest, no longer possible to ask this question and expect it to be answered in view of what we already know about the way that we are made.

On these two points we have yet much discussion — and for the moment I shall just give it back to Waddington — perhaps to befriend the oranges or perhaps to answer one of these deeper questions.

WADDINGTON

Well no, I think I will leave the deeper question to the others and perhaps, later, all of us. I just want to say about the idea that chreods are a vitalistic conception, that is really not so at all. The idea of a chreod is simply of the same kind as the idea of a homeostatic system, as used by the cyberneticians. Really biologists invented the idea of homeostasis long before electrical engineers got around to inventing the word 'cybernetics'; it is a well-known notion that goes back to the late nineteenth century. An embryologist like myself enlarged this idea to include a time dimension, and a chreod is very like a homeostatic system, only it is going along a pathway in time. Most engineers, and most of the early biologists were only concerned with holding something steady, but I think this is inadequate for many things in biology. I don't think you can leave out that change in time and still have an adequately flexible notion. But the notion of a chreod, or a stabilised pathway or a canalised pathway, or whatever you like to call it, is not vitalistic at all but is just the same sort of thing as a homeostatic system.

Again I think we may come back to the question of teleology. All I will say at the moment is that the reason why most animals behave as they do is that they find it advantageous in competition with others, and natural selection has tailored them to do it.

LONGUET-HIGGINS

Well, I want first of all to disown a view which is sufficiently different from my own for me to disagree with it, and that is 'it's all in the Schrodinger equation'. If I ever said that I certainly didn't mean the Schrodinger equation is enough for us in answering interesting and important questions at higher levels. To say that it is all implicit in the Schrodinger equation is quite a different thing from saying that with the aid of the

41

Schrodinger equation we can solve all problems in chemistry, biology, sociology, and economics. And I hoped I had made it clear last time that that was my general view.

Well, having said that, may I come to John Lucas' question which I think is a fair question in relation to Waddington's paper. 'How are reasons possible; how can we discuss giving reasons for doing something?' I would have thought that that was not an insuperably difficult problem if one thinks about examining the output – if I may refer again to computer programs – examining the output of a computer program, finding a somewhat puzzling set of symbols, and then enquiring, as one can, 'Why did it print these out?' One answers the question by referring back to the program and seeing the various choices that were made at the various stages, according to various circumstances, and examining why the circumstances were that way at that time, and referring to the program to note that if x was equal to 2 at that time then y would have to be given the value of 3 – or something like that. One can in fact discuss the reasons why something worked out the way it did in relation to computer programs. I wouldn't feel insulted if somebody said the reason why I used the word – some word that I might have just picked up from Waddington in the course of this conversation – was that I had just heard it from Waddington. I would not be insulted. I would think that was a perfectly good reason, a penetrating observation on what was going on in my mind.

One further point I would like to raise with Wad is something that he might well have said himself if he had had time. I very much like his idea of there being various valleys in this so-called epigenetic landscape, a valley being essentially one of these chreods down which the river flows, changing its course within limits – limits set by the banks of that valley. But I would like to reinforce his idea that ways of behaving are essentially chreods between which we have got to choose and that a very small influence from outside or inside may make all the difference. One might, for example, catch sight of something out of the corner of one's eye and say something entirely different from what one would otherwise have said. The immense sensitivity of the human being to minute perturbations from outside is enough of a reason for asserting that any attempt to predict people's behaviour in detail is doomed to failure; and of course the idea of doing so doesn't really make sense anyway when we come to discuss human affairs.

KENNY

I'd like to make two points about Waddington's paper. Firstly I don't think that freewill is the kind of thing he thinks it is and secondly I don't think that consciousness is the kind of thing that he thinks it is.

Waddington believes that to have freewill is to have certain kinds of experiences — pretty unpleasant experiences to judge by his reference to the puritan tradition and those last few seconds before breasting the tape. Now I think that to have freewill is to be able to do things when you want to and to be able not to do them if you don't want to. It is a matter of a certain sort of capacity or ability or power; it isn't a matter of a particular experience. Sometimes we feel that we can do things when we want to and we are wrong, other times we can do things when we want to and we don't have any special feeling about it. Whether one feels one has freewill is quite a different question from whether one has it or not.

Now, secondly, I think that consciousness is not the private thing which is unamenable to scientific treatment that Waddington thinks it is. When I say that consciousness is not particularly private I don't mean to be propounding anything very difficult or metaphysical. I simply mean that I can tell by watching other people behave whether or not they are conscious, and I can tell by looking at this mug that it isn't conscious and I know that this mug is not conscious as certainly as I know anything. I was slightly disappointed that Waddington came to the conclusion that atoms and molecules were probably not conscious. I thought from his initial remarks about the sex-life of proteins that we were perhaps going to come to a conclusion, which he seemed to defend the other day, that consciousness is widely spread throughout the universe. It certainly seems to me that it is quite consistent with the view that consciousness is something private which we can never really make contact with except in our own case that this mug should be conscious. What on Waddington's view is wrong with the idea that, for all we know, this mug may be in excruciating pain? Of course we have to combine with this the supposition that the excruciatingness of its pain is only matched by the stoic quality of its fortitude. But it seems to me that on the view that Waddington has put forward there would be nothing nonsensical about that supposition. Against this, I think that consciousness, like freewill, is a matter of having certain sorts of ability. To be conscious is, for instance, to see and hear. Whether somebody can see or hear is a matter of whether he can discriminate between certain things, and whether he can discriminate between certain things is something that we can test both in simple everyday ways and in complicated experimental ways. Consciousness is therefore something which can be tested; it isn't something that is private and unamenable to scientific treatment.

WADDINGTON

I want to make a reply to some of the points just made by Kenny. Now, I am not a bit certain that the mug is not a little conscious. I said that I think you have to add to the definition of atoms something to do with consciousness, but I added that this consciousness is not going to be as highly evolved as ours;

I feel that it would be somehow akin to it, some kind of beginnings of it, as much simplified compared to our consciousness as our structure is more complicated than that of an atom. I am definitely not ruling out that there is some sort of thing allied to consciousness all through the world.

Then this question of the privacy of consciousness. I think that one of the routes which may enable us to approach this is now becoming a fashionable experience, though not so much in scientific circles: namely, experimentation with what tend to be called novel forms of consciousness. If everybody's got the same sort of consciousness, there is not much you can say about it — except have you got it or haven't you got it? But if people start getting funny states of consciousness, by breathing exercises and yoga positions, or LSD if you like, and if they can communicate — which they do seem to be able to do, so I gather — to communicate something about these to other people, and in fact train people to get into specific states of consciousness, then I think this phenomenon is becoming more amenable to scientific study. I carefully said — I am always hedging my bets, I'm afraid — that consciousness was *pretty* private; but I'm not excluding that it may also be *somewhat* public.

On this point that freewill is the ability to act when you want to or to do what you like, I just think we differ on this. I may will to go to the Ritz, but if I haven't a five pound note in my pocket I can't do it; the ability to do something doesn't seem to me to be at all the same thing as consciously willing to do it. Again, you have to remember the terrific number of things you do when you are not consciously willing to do them; you do them as a spontaneous reaction to an input; or you want to answer the telephone and you just run down the stairs — a terrifically complex performance carried out by your cerebellum, but you aren't really conscious of doing it. I don't consider that as something that poses the problem of freewill. That merely poses the problem of the mechanisms of the wiring circuits in your cerebellum, which is quite a different kettle of fish.

Fourth Lecture. Determinism and Mind

Having said last night that I disagreed with the account of
freewill given by Waddington there is some obligation on me
to offer some sort of alternative account. I think that
Waddington was quite right to stress the importance of the
freedom of the will as one of the unique characteristics of
human beings. But traditionally to the question 'are human
beings unique, and if so in what ways?' there have been at least
two different answers. One of them is that only human beings
are independent, autonomous, and free, but the other is that
only human beings use language. I want to talk about these
two answers. Are they in competition or do they complement
each other? Is autonomy essential to a language user? Is the
mastery of language essential to an autonomous agent?

Recently the uniqueness of man as a language user has been
much emphasized by the linguists of the school of Chomsky.
It has been challenged from two sides. There are those who
deny that the natural ability to use language is peculiar to
human beings among animal species, and they point to the
striking success of the Chimpanzee Washoe in mimicking
American sign language. On the other hand, the protagonists
of artificial intelligence claim to be able to program computers
to use and understand natural languages. There are now in
existence, not too far from here, systems which are claimed by
their designers to be capable of understanding some bits of
normal English, and elsewhere there are systems which are
claimed to be capable of answering questions, executing
commands, and entering into dialogues. Now if these claims
are correct then human beings must agree that not only
animals but also non-living artifacts can share the ability to
speak a language. Not even the warmest admirers of non-
human animals and of computers commonly regard them as
fully autonomous agents. Animals may be lively, cunning, or
independent but we don't credit them with moral responsibility. And on the other hand the most successful of the
artificial intelligence systems run on principles which are
wholly deterministic. It appears therefore either that autonomy is unnecessary for language use, or that the appearance
which animals and computers give of using language is an
illusory one.

Since the time of Hobbes, philosophers have long considered, either with favour or with contempt, the suggestion
that indeterminism is not essential for autonomy. A decision
on this age-long debate wouldn't by itself settle whether

autonomy and the use of language necessarily go together. But it may well throw light on the relationship between the two if we take the traditional discussion of the relation between autonomy and indeterminism a step further.

At first sight there seems to be a clear conflict between determinism and freedom. You will remember that because of this apparent conflict Dr Johnson rejected determinism: 'We know our will is free and there's an end on it', he said. If we add his hidden premise, we have the simple argument: freedom and determinism are incompatible; we know we are free; therefore determinism is false.

Now philosophers who have rejected the incompatibility between determinism and freedom have commonly made a distinction between various senses of freedom. They have admitted that there are senses in which freedom is incompatible with determinism but they have denied that we know in those senses that we are free. The sense in which we know we are free, they say, is one in which freedom leaves room for determinism.

An early distinction of this kind which was long influential was the distinction between liberty of indifference and liberty of spontaneity. This began as a theological distinction. It was used by people like Jonathan Edwards, who were committed to determinism by their admiration for Calvin. It was later used also by people like Hume who were committed to determinism by admiration for Newton. The concept of liberty of spontaneity is one which approaches freewill through the notion of desire or wanting. It sees the exercise of freewill essentially as the execution of one's wants. To act freely is to act because one wants to. This was the notion I was using last night. It doesn't of course mean, as Waddington seemed to suggest, that to enjoy freedom of spontaneity is to be able to do everything that one wants, but it is to be able in some cases to put one's wants into execution. Now the notion of liberty of indifference does not start from 'wanting', it starts from 'power' or 'ability'. It sees freewill as essentially a capacity for alternative action. To act freely on this view is to act in possession of the power to act otherwise. It is only liberty of indifference that presents an obvious contrast with determinism. The contradictory of spontaneity is not determinism but compulsion.

The two types of liberty appear to be distinct and in theory separable. And once the distinction has been drawn it seems easy enough for the defender of determinism to reply to Dr Johnson's simple argument. The freedom which is incompatible with determinism, he can say, is liberty of indifference. The freedom which we know we have is liberty of spontaneity. Whether we enjoy liberty of indifference can't be just a matter of bluff commonsense experience. How could experience show us that there is no sufficient antecedent condition for our actions: that our actions are uncaused? Whether there are such causal conditions depends on the nature of the totality of physical laws which govern life in our Universe. How could the introspection even of Dr Johnson be sufficient to establish the nature of those? How could one feel within oneself the lack of a law correlating one's present action with one's previous history and environment? In another pronouncement Johnson said: 'All theory is against the freedom of the will; all experience is for it'. But what all theory is against is liberty of indifference; what experience is for is liberty of spontaneity.

The theory which I have been presenting so far might be called compatibilism, that is to say the theory that freedom and determinism are compatible with each other. It is sometimes known as soft determinism. Now the difficulty with compatibilist theory as put forward by a writer such as Hume is that it involves a naive conception of mental causation. The determinism which is put forward is a psychological determinism. It is observed that the fact that we can do what we want doesn't mean that we can want what we want. If all our wants are determined, the theory goes, then it may be true that we can do whatever we want and yet all our actions can still be determined. Now the theory hasn't lacked defenders in this form in the present century. But I think that at the present time most philosophers would regard it as incorrect to think of wants, or desires, or decisions, or the will, as being some sort of mental event which causally determines an action. To say that somebody did an act because he wanted to is not to postulate a mental event as the cause of the action operating through some mental mechanism which we don't yet perfectly understand. There are of course some wants which are mental events: pangs of hunger, stirrings of lust or sudden impulses to pick a flower. Nonetheless the wanting which makes an act voluntary, the wanting which makes the difference between voluntariness and non-voluntariness, is not a mental event. Take a simple example. The sentence that I have just uttered I uttered voluntarily. I chose each word of it, but there wasn't any mental event of desiring to utter the word, no act of willing, between each word and the next, to choose the next word. If some voluntary events, like the choice of words, don't demand a specific event to cause them why should any?

Now certainly when one says that somebody brought about a certain result because he wanted to, one is saying something about the causation of the result. But what one is saying is not that the act was caused by a certain mental event, but rather that the agent was in a certain state in relation to causes when he did it. I think that it is a statement essentially about the absence of certain causes or certain circumstances. This idea is a very old one; it goes back to Aristotle. Aristotle thought that to say that an act was voluntary was to say that it wasn't done

47

under constraint or by mistake. I think that Aristotle's list of the conditions which must be absent is certainly too short and I must confess I don't know how to complete it. But one can criticise Aristotle on this point without agreeing with the proponents of liberty of indifference that in order to be voluntary, an act must be totally uncaused.

The proponents of liberty of spontaneity are right to say that a person's doing x because he wants to is compatible with the causal pre-determination of the event which is his doing x. But this isn't because his wanting to do x is itself a cause which is causally determined. It is rather because the types of causal determinism that are ruled out by saying that a man acted voluntarily don't necessarily exhaust the types of determinism that there are. Pre-eminent among the types of causal determinism that are ruled out are psychological determinisms — by which I mean determinisms in virtue of laws which can only be stated by the use of mental predicates. This includes economic and sociological determinism. But physiological determinism is a rather different thing. It seems to me to be neither entailed nor excluded by the existence of liberty of spontaneity. It seems to me that there is no incompatibility between explanation by neuro-physiological states and explanations in terms of wants and intentions. And this is so even if the laws of neuro-physiology should turn out in the end to be fundamentally deterministic — this may or may not be likely.

There is one objection, an important objection, which is always made to this soft determinist theory. It is made by John Lucas in his book *The Freedom of the Will*. It was made recently by Professor Anscombe in her inaugural lecture at the University of Cambridge. My actions are mostly physical movements, the objection goes, and if these physical movements are physically pre-determined by processes which I do not control, then my freedom is illusory. So the truth of physical determinism is indispensable if we are to make anything of the claim to freedom. Now I think that this protest can be attacked on purely logical grounds. The protester's argument appeals to the principle — sometimes known as Leibniz's law — that if x is identical with y then whatever is true of x is also true of y. My actions are identical with certain physical movements — the argument goes — these physical movements are determined, therefore my actions are determined. But it's well-known that Leibniz's law cannot be relied on in modal contexts — that is to say, in contexts where the predicates in question involve the notions of necessity and possibility. To take a simple example, the number of member nations in the Common Market is identical with the number six and the number six is necessarily smaller than the number seven, but the number of members of the Common Market is not necessarily smaller than seven. It is only contingently so at

48

this time. But now, the predicate 'determined' like the predicate 'necessarily smaller than' is a modal predicate. That is, to say that an event was determined is to say that there was no possibility of things turning out otherwise.

This reply to the incompatibilist is suggested by recent work of the American philosopher Donald Davidson. Davidson's own solution to the question of the relationship between freedom and determinism is to say that while being *caused* is a relationship which links events in themselves, being *determined* is a property which attaches to events under certain descriptions. For an event to be determined is for it to fall under a description such that there exists a law from which with certain antecedent conditions it could be deduced that an event of that description would occur. For Davidson, events are part of the furniture of the world in a way in which laws are not. According to his theory, laws are essentially linguistic.

Now this Davidsonian answer to the type of position represented by Lucas and Anscombe does not seem to me to be conclusive. Laws may perhaps be linguistic, I don't know, but natural possibilities and impossibilities are surely not linguistic. To take an instance of natural impossibility, 'I cannot fly'. Now this is not a property which belongs to me only under some descriptions and not under others. However you describe me, whatever description you use of me, it is true that I cannot fly.

Now the necessity and possibility which is commonly formalised in logic — in the area of logic known as 'modal logic' which deals with these questions — is essentially logical necessity — the necessity which attaches to logical truths. Many philosophers have believed that logical necessity is ultimately a kind of linguistic necessity. If they are right then the failure of Leibniz's law in modal contexts may be ultimately a linguistic phenomenon from which no lesson can be drawn about non-linguistic necessities and possibilities. I don't myself believe that logical necessity is essentially a matter of language, and quite apart from this there are good reasons for thinking that the 'cans' and the 'musts' of natural necessity and possibility are not adequately represented by any of the standard modal logics. I shall list some of these reasons in a moment. But first I want to draw attention to the significance of these logical considerations for our overall purpose.

The reason for going into elementary matters of formal logic is this. The expression of deterministic theory demands the use of the notion of natural necessity and possibility; the reporting of free actions demands the use of the notion of rational or mind-guided possibility — and whatever the relation this latter type of possibility may have to the former we clearly need a formal logic for natural necessity and possibility. If we have not yet a logic adequate to formalize these notions then it seems that we are not yet in a position to know how to set about constructing a computer programme to simulate the activity of an autonomous agent.

The basis of contemporary developments in formal logic over the last century is the first order predicate calculus — the part of logic which deals with predicates of objects and quantifiers (the symbols which correspond to the words 'all' and 'some' in ordinary English). This first order predicate calculus is a system of considerable power whose properties are by now very well known. John Lucas will be talking about some of them tomorrow. Among the things which are known about it is that it is inadequate for the description of human mental states and activities. Human mental states, like belief and desire, have a certain logical property known as 'intentionality': they are intentional. When we say that beliefs and desires are intentional in this logical sense, we mean that there are various principles of reasoning which are valid in the first order predicate calculus, and which will lead from true premises to false conclusions if they are applied to the thoughts and wants of human beings. The best known of such principles is once again Leibniz's law — the law that if x is the same as y then whatever is true of x is true of y. This law fails in intentional contexts no less than in modal contexts. Suppose that a detective knows that Mr Hyde is a murderer and suppose that Dr Jekyll is identical with Mr Hyde; still it does not follow that the detective knows that Dr Jekyll is a murderer. So Leibniz's law in such cases does not hold.

Since the failure of Leibniz's law occurs both in modal contexts and in intentional contexts it might be thought that modal logics would be adequate for the description of human activities and capacities. But a number of arguments make it clear that standard modal logics do not suffice to formalise even the simpler statements about human abilities and capacities. In standard modal logics, the following three laws which I am about to enunciate appear either as axioms or as theorems:

1. If p then possibly p.
2. It is possible that either p or q if and only if either it is possible that p or it is possible that q.
3. If it is possible that it is possible that p then it is possible that p.

I think you will agree that these principles sound harmless enough. If you have any objection to them it will be on the grounds of tediousness rather than of falsehood. But if modal logic of this kind is to be able to formalise statements about human abilities and skills then we have to be able to translate a sentence like 'I can do such and such' into the form 'it is possible that I am doing such and such,' and vice versa. So that 'I can whistle the Emperor Concerto from beginning to end' has to be 'it is possible that I am . . . etc.' Now once we allow this transformation it's obvious that these three laws can very

50

easily be falsified.

Take the first one. I can't spell the word 'seize'. I can never remember whether or not it is an exception to the rule about 'i' before 'e' yet since I usually toss a coin to decide how to order the vowels, from time to time I spell it correctly. So on any particular occasion it is true that I am spelling 'seize' correctly, and yet it is not true that I can spell 'seize' correctly. So 'if p then possibly p' is falsified.

For an example of the falsification of the second law, consider the case of my two friends, Tweedledum and Tweedledee. They are identical twins, they look totally unlike anybody else that I know, so that when I meet one or other of them I can always tell that it is either Tweedledum or Tweedledee but I can never tell either that it is Tweedledum or that it is Tweedledee and so that provides a counter instance to the second one.

Finally, law number three. It is hard to translate this one at all into an ordinary 'can' sentence because it is not clear what is meant by 'I can can do x'. The only plausible sense seems to be 'I can acquire the ability to do x'. If it is so interpreted then this law is quite false. Suppose that I am filling in a questionnaire for a job and it says 'Can you speak Russian?' I argue that I have the ability to acquire the ability to speak Russian and if it is possible that it is possible that p then it is possible that p so I answer 'yes' to the question.

For these reasons and for others which it would take too long to detail it seems to me clear that modal logic of the classical kind is inadequate to deal with the capacities of human beings. I should say that I have not chosen these laws just randomly as things to find fault with. They are the three axioms of a particular well-known system.

Now let us return to the incompatibilist argument favoured by Mr Lucas, that if our actions are identical with physical movements which are determined, then our actions are themselves determined. Whether this argument is valid or not depends on whether the predicates which are involved in the statement of determinism and freedom are predicates to which Leibniz's law applies. If the argument I have just gone through is correct then we can't argue from the analogy of modal logic that the law doesn't apply, because the 'cans' and 'musts' of determinism and freedom are not those which are formalised by modal logics. However, there are independent reasons for thinking that these 'cans' and 'musts' are not subject to Leibniz's law as they must be if the incompatibilist argument is to work.

Here is a formal argument which looks all right until you begin to think about it. 'I can do x, doing x is doing y, therefore I can do y'. This argument does work in some cases, namely if it is some sort of logical truth that doing x is doing y, if it is true by definition. But it doesn't work if all that is meant by this second premise is that a particular instance of doing x is the same as a particular instance of doing y. Let me explain what I mean. Given a dart I can usually hit the dart board. Now on a particular occasion I may hit the dart board by hitting the centre of the board, but it by no means follows that I am capable of hitting the centre of the board. I am not. Any particular exercise of a power or a skill will have other descriptions besides the one which occurs in the specification of the power, and the possession of the power which is specified in no way involves the possession of the power to perform acts according to those other descriptions. The example I have given concerns a human skill, but similar considerations apply to natural possibilities and necessities. I conclude, therefore, that the argument to say that freedom and determinism are incompatible, which is based on arguments of this form, is invalid.

To argue, as I have been doing, for the compatibility of freedom and determinism is in effect to say that liberty of spontaneity does not involve liberty of indifference, at least if liberty of indifference is interpreted in any way which entails indeterminism. But it may well be that the two kinds of liberty are connected in a subtle way. Aristotle thought that it was only when an agent was of a kind to be able both to do x and not to do x that you could attribute a want or desire to do x as opposed to a mere tendency to do x. This may be true, but even if it is it doesn't follow, I think, that when somebody performs a certain action this can't be explained by saying he wanted to do it unless on that occasion it was in his power not to do it. To take a very old example, somebody may stay in a room because he wants to, even though unknown to himself the door has been locked the whole time. But the notion of power which is involved in the definition of freedom of indifference doesn't seem to me on reflection to be one which is incompatible with predictability, much less with determinism. On particular occasions it may well be true that I can do x even if it is predictable that I will not do x. There is nothing contradictory in saying that I can, but will not, do x any more than there is anything contradictory in saying that I could have done x but did not do so. Thirty seconds ago I did not throw the chalk into the third row of the audience. But I could have done, and my not having done so did not take away the power which I then had. The presupposition which I have so far accepted uncriticised from Hume, namely the presupposition that liberty of indifference is incompatible with determinism, is a presupposition which won't, once looked at, bear very much weight.

At last I want to return to the topic of artificial intelligence. At the beginning of this paper I argued that it seemed at first sight an objection to artificial language-using systems that they were deterministic systems. If my argument this evening has been right, then it seems that this is not a valid objection. Even in the case of human language-users, indeterminism doesn't seem to be established. *A fortiori* there is no reason to demand that if a computer is to be regarded as possessing the ability to use language it should be exempt from determinism. But since we can't be certain that liberty of indifference can be equated with indeterminism it remains an open question whether liberty of indifference of some kind is necessary for the ability to use language. In saying this I think I am allying myself with Waddington in thinking that the questions about Heisenberg indeterminacy are really irrelevant to questions about the freedom of the human will.

Though I think that their being deterministic is no reason why computer systems should not be genuinely said to use language, I think that alleged language-using computers, such as those using the programmes I know about, cannot genuinely be said to be using language. Because even if liberty of indifference is not necessary for a language-user, liberty of spontaneity — the ability to do things because one wants to — does seem to me to be essential. That is to say, only agents who have the power to select their own goals, and to act in pursuit of those goals, can be said to use language. Because it is essential, in order to use language, to be able to confer meaning on symbols; and meaning can only be conferred by agents who are capable of having common purposes and a shared form of life. Of course, the output of a computer which is programmed to produce English sentences is a meaningful output, but the meaning is conferred on it not by the computer itself, but by the living human beings who use the English language.

Liberty of spontaneity is something which artificial intelligences lack. They can perhaps be said to have goals, and perhaps even self-selected goals. If a computer is programmed to parse English sentences when a particular sentence is typed into it then it may perhaps be said to select the parsing of that sentence as a goal, and the choice of that goal governs a large number of complicated sub-routines. But it seems clear that computers don't have the long-term self-selected goals which constitute a form of life as the necessary background to a use of language. To see this, consider that if there were a number of computers isolated from human contact, which had an output isomorphic to the alleged language-using computers this would not be sufficient to make their output into a use of language. If we are tempted to think otherwise, it's simply because their output in present circumstances is one which is interpreted as a language and connects with our human life and behaviour. But for something to be a language it is not enough that it should have a certain complicated mathematical structure. It is essential that that structure should be interpreted and interpretation — the conveying of meaning on symbols — is so far the prerogative of human beings.

Discussion

WADDINGTON

Kenny has given us an extremely dense paper with a great many precisely formulated arguments. There is only time to make a very few short comments. He has dealt with two distinct problems, between which he makes connections, and — I am not quite certain I entirely follow his connections. First, he dealt with the problem of determinism and freewill, and then he came to the question of the use of language, by computers for instance. Now on the question of determinism and freewill, he first of all made a distinction between the liberty of indifference, which says 'I did something but I could have done something else'; and, as he says, this is really incompatible with a belief in determinism. Then he contrasted this with the liberty of spontaneity which says 'I did this because I wanted to,' and he then pursued the arguments — is this, or is this not, compatible with determinism? At first he gave some arguments tending to show that it might well be compatible but then he came to the gist of his thesis, a point which was his main argument against allowing that even the liberty of spontaneity is compatible with determinism. This argument is that my actions are mostly physical movements, and if these movements are physically pre-determined by processes which I do not control, then my freedom is illusory; and therefore physical determinism is incompatible with liberty of spontaneity.

He then went on to ways in which this conclusion might possibly be escaped. He described a system of what he called 'modal logic' which rejects what he spoke of as Leibniz's law, that 'if x is identical with y whatever is true of x is also true of y'. He expounded this possible way of escape, but really, I think, came to the conclusion that it could not work — that it did not really give you an escape from the argument. My criticism of this part of his argument was that it all boiled down, at least in the way it was expounded here, to translating these arguments into terms involving words such as 'can' and 'must' and words of that kind. Now these are notoriously ambiguous words — 'I *can* do something' Kenny interpreted to mean 'It is possible that I am doing it', but it could also be 'It is not impossible that I shall do it'; it could also be 'I am permitted to do it'; and it could be 'I know how to do it regularly'. And this brings me to what I think is one of my major criticisms: that he tended to try to refute arguments by what I should call once-off examples. For instance, he refers to the argument 'I can do x, doing x is the same as doing y and therefore I can do y'. Then later he took as an example, playing darts; and if he threw a dart and he did actually once

54

hit the Bull's Eye, then he could certainly say 'I can hit the board'. But suppose someone came to me and said 'I'll take you on at a game of darts for a double scotch against a half-pint and I'm just a beginner − I can hit the board', and if he did hit the Bull's Eye first shot − well, I possibly would begin to wonder. And if he went on regularly hitting the Bull's Eye, I shouldn't accept those odds again the next time. Kenny stated at one point that there was something called the 'first order predicate calculus', and this included words such as 'some' and 'all' but it seemed to me noticeable that in the arguments he expounded the words 'some' and 'all' were not included. He doesn't say that 'I can sometimes do x' or 'I can always do x'; he just says 'I can do x'. And then he gives one example of doing x, when doing x is not the same as doing y. Now obviously I will have to study these arguments a lot more carefully than I have yet had time to − but it seemed to me that Kenny was rejecting arguments because he formulated them without any specification of whether a relation holds once, sometimes or always, and then he could give one example when it didn't hold. So I am still rather sceptical about his escape from the argument that liberty of spontaneity is incompatible with determinism. He argued that you could escape from it but I think this escape was based on a failure to specify in his arguments whether he was dealing with a regular occurrence or an irregular occurrence. I personally think you may be able to escape from it, but in quite a different way.

Now, turning to his other argument, about language and the liberty of spontaneity, he claimed at one point that only agents that can select their own goals and act in pursuit of these goals can be said to use language. Here I think it is a question of the word 'use'. Slaves can't select their own goals but have to do what they are told − and they can certainly use language well enough. I think what Kenny was talking about here is a very important thing, but it is not so much the use of language as the ability to invent a language. At the end of his paper he speaks of a number of computers, isolated from human contact, which have an output isomorphic with the language-using computers, and argues that this would not be sufficient to justify saying they were using language. Well, I think it would be sufficient for us to say they were using language, but it wouldn't be sufficient for us to say they had invented it. If they were using English they would be using English; and if the computers could understand each other, and each do what others, were telling them, they wouldn't have invented the language but they would be using it, in my opinion.

LUCAS

I think I ought to pick up the gauntlet which was thrown down and I want to start by being slightly unfair and making a debating point against Dr Kenny. He has wished on me and

55

Professor Anscombe an argument which if it were valid would support a conclusion which we both maintain. He then points out that the argument is invalid and from this invites you to draw the conclusion that the conclusion that we draw is not true. I want to go a bit further, though: first of all, even if Kenny could make a rather stronger point, I think I should still be rather unworried because it is one of the theses that I am committed to maintaining, − and have maintained − successfully − that no formal system of inference can capture all the inferences which we regard as valid. So that even if there were some informal inference which could not be formalised in S4 or in the predicate calculus, nevertheless it would not follow that this inference was not valid. But I want to go one stage further because I am very unhappy with the sorrows of the policeman in London not knowing whether Dr Jekyll is the same as Mr Hyde, or, to take a more classical and more local example, the worry of George IV in Edinburgh, who wanted to know whether Scott was the author of *Waverley*. And the argument which Kenny has put forward is that George IV did know, presumably, that the author of *Waverley* was the author of *Waverley*, and this is a necessary truth, but although it is true that George IV knew that the author of *Waverley* was the author of *Waverley* and it is true that Scott was the author of *Waverley*, he didn't know that Scott was the author of *Waverley*. But let me take another example. George IV might have wanted to know whether the author of *Waverley* was the author of *Old Mortality* or of *Ivanhoe*, or of many others, and from the fact that he did not know that Scott was the author of *Waverley* it would not at all follow that he could not have known that the author of *Waverley* was the author of *Ivanhoe*. After all, it might very well have had on the title page of one of these 'by the author of *Waverley*'. And this is the case in the argument that I am putting forward. I can't formalise it, because it uses two sorts of modality. Essentially, what I am claiming is that the connection between the description of a piece of behaviour which is something which physicists or physiologists might be able to discuss, whether it is determined or not, and the description of a human action is not *that* contingent. That is to say, although it may not be in the same modality as that used by the Laplacean physicists who from a given initial description of the universe and knowing the laws of mechanics could have predicted the final positions and momenta of all the Newtonian corpuscles − although it might not be the same as that modality, depending on some physical necessity, still there is some necessity of being able to work out from description of behaviour, not perhaps the exact description of action but at least some descriptions of action. Take for example the hypothetical action of Kenny in throwing a piece of chalk into the third row of the audience. Now, if we had been able to predict that he would have done this, we might not have been able to say with certainty whether this action which was being described to us was a philosophical example or as an existentialist doing an *acte gratuit*, but at least we could have been sure that this was not an exercise in Buddhist impassivity, and we would have known that with some sort of modal necessity. We should have to have a much more complicated modal logic than that which is offered on the board, with at least two sorts of modal operator, m and m', and what the laws of that modal logic would be I should hesitate to have to say, but I think I can be reasonably sure that if I have got 'necessarily p' according to one modality and 'necessarily (according to another modality) p is identical with q' then 'necessarily (according to one or other of those modalities or some other modality still) q'. Well, this is my half answer to Kenny.

Let me just make one more positive point. He was maintaining that the liberty of spontaneity was not the same as the liberty of indifference, which is of course true, and that the liberty of spontaneity was the only thing which we need be worried about with freewill and is compatible with determinism. But this won't wash. He defines the liberty of spontaneity in terms of some sort of ability to do what one wants. But supposing someone here had been hypnotised, by, say Kenny, into throwing back that piece of chalk and then did it. Now it is clear that he wanted to do it and it is clear that in many senses he was free to do it — he had the liberty of that apparently spontaneous action of throwing back the piece of chalk! — but we would not say that he was really free to do it, and if the matter came to the court of law the fact that he had been hypnotised would be evidence against holding him responsible. Or to take another example — the sad cases of men born with xyy chromosomes; insofar as it is made out that people with this genetic constitution cannot but be rather too tall and rather too violent, they are acquitted of criminal responsibility. We don't hold kleptomaniacs responsible. We don't think that they are free. Although they undoubtedly want to steal, and can do what they want, the whole point is that they are not free not to want to steal and this is the issue of the freedom of the will on which I am taking my stand and which seems to be more fundamental than the many true and important things that Kenny has said.

LONGUET-HIGGINS

I don't really want to take more than a minute because I think Kenny ought to have the chance of replying to what has already been said. I think Waddington was very unfair to Kenny. I don't think that he really said at all what Wad suggested but any way I would like to take up Kenny's question whether we could speak of language use without the language-user having selected his own goals. I thought Waddington made a correct point when he said that one couldn't really speak of the proper use of language unless the language was interpreted. But that is a different question from whether the language-user has selected his own goals or not. Now it seems to me that if you say 'Please move out of the way', and I pick up my chair and move out of the way, you know that I am at least understanding what you said, – that your language has been interpreted by me. But I might not have selected my own goals; I might have been a robot to which you addressed this remark, and a robot in fact could very well do that kind of thing – or so I am told. And so I want to insist that we must separate, in our discussion of what counts as a real language-user, the question of the self-selection of goals – which is of course a very interesting business – and the question of the interpretation of utterances in the language, which I think is something we can claim to have made a start on already.

KENNY

I would like to begin by thanking Waddington for his summary of what I said, which I thought was very accurate up to the final point which I would like to thank Longuet-Higgins for mentioning. I do think that the line of argument that I followed gives you an escape from the argument to show that freedom and determinism are incompatible. I do think we can escape from the Lucas argument. Lucas was, of course, quite right that I hadn't proved that the two were compatible. I don't quite know how one can prove the compatibility of two things save by disproving the arguments that are brought up to show they are incompatible, and I await with interest the further arguments to show that they are incompatible.

I agree with Waddington that the ability to do something can be displayed by doing it regularly. But I don't think that it is sufficiently established by a single exercise of a certain skill. Now the examples that I gave, as several speakers pointed out, were on the whole rather out of the way examples, and of course they were just single examples. But the point of my argument was this: that the Anscombe-Lucas argument appeals tacitly to a certain logical law and that logical law doesn't work. Now if a logical law is to work it must work always. It is no good saying 'Oh, I know in that example that you gave it didn't work but I can think of lots of other examples where it would work – just look at Scott and the author of *Waverley*'. If something really is a logical law then it always works and a single counter-example is enough to overthrow it.

John Lucas was perfectly correct in what he said about hypnotism – that action under hypnotic suggestion is not free. Hypnotism was one of the things which I had in mind when I said that I thought Aristotle's definition of voluntariness was inadequate. He said that an action was voluntary if it was not done under duress or by mistake. I said I thought his list of the things that must be absent was too short, and I would certainly agree with John that hypnosis is one of the things that has to be absent. About the xyy chromosomes, I am not sure — I would like to hear more about them because I have heard slightly different accounts of the data from the one Lucas gave.

Finally, with regard to Longuet-Higgins' remarks, I would not wish to claim that in order for somebody to be a language-user he has to select every goal off his own bat — clearly this would be far too strong a claim. It is only that in order to be a language-user you do have to be capable of choosing your own long-term goals. Why do I think this? Because I think that the interpretation, the giving of meaning to language is ultimately a matter of intentions. If one is to mean something by something then one has to intend to produce certain effects, and so on. I am not yet convinced that, clever as they are, Longuet-Higgins' computers have intentions. But this is a topic we shall return to.

Fifth Lecture. The Autonomy of Mind

Under the title, the Autonomy of Mind, I am going to discuss two theses. First a negative and contentious one, and then a positive, perhaps less contentious but rather more cloudy, one. The negative one I think in this place should be reckoned as being largely addressed against David Hume, who put himself out as the Newton of the mind and was going to give us some very clear rules governing the operation of the human mind. What I am going to offer should be seen, as it were, as another essay on the intellectual powers of man.

I want to contrast certain different types of reasoning, different types of understanding. And since intellectuals seldom tell the truth except when they are trying to be rude, I want you to go for a moment, in thought, to the Senate of a university — not here of course — but another senate where the professors are quarrelling. Quarrelling about money. Each professor wants a rather bigger share of the available money to expand his own Department, because each professor knows that his own subject is best; and behind the interchange of incivilities certain themes will come out and particularly one between the arts men and the scientists. The scientists will complain that the arts men are sloppy and subjective; they waffle away; they are little better, really, than journalists, and you have got no clear sense that what they are doing can be established as clearly and objectively true. As one particular case comes up; who shall be, say, a Reader in Ecclesiastical History — x or y? They are both going to be writing about the covenanting movement in South West Scotland, x is an episcopalian and y is a presbyterian, and this matters: whereas there is no such thing as Episcopalian, Presbyterian, Wee Free or even Humanist, Chemistry. The arts men, in return, complain that the scientists are terribly narrow, or, if they are very young, they say that they are irrelevant. They keep on plodding along, examining the sex-life of woodlice, answering questions which nobody really wants to ask, and failing to see the point of this objection and that objection. Unable to take the longer view or without the larger vision, and terribly much lacking in intuitive insight.

Well, I shall not develop this very much, partly because as I came up on the plane I found that it was done very much better in a book I was reading, G. H. vón Wright's *Explanation and Understanding*, (Routledge and Kegan Paul, 1971) and the first chapter foreclosed a lot of what I was going to say by doing it better. Partly, also, because this distinction seems now to be conceded by all of us here; and rather than say things which are agreeable, my function is to say things which are disagreeable, and I am going to try to pick a quarrel with the other three which is not whether there is a distinction but whether this distinction is irreducible. After all, it is a long time since it was originally noticed – Plato in the *Phaedrus* (263a) draws a distinction something like this in terms of a decision-procedure. Controversies about whether someone is good or just, he says, go on for ever, whereas whether something is made of iron or silver, is a matter which can be settled definitively. Pascal drew a distinction between *l'esprit de finesse*, and *l'esprit de géométrie*. In the last century Newman in this country, and Droysen and Dilthey in Germany, kept on reiterating that there was another sort of understanding besides that which could be squeezed into Hume's canons or those of the purely mathematical sciences. Nevertheless, this penny has not dropped. Even when I was an undergraduate I was made to read a very important and influential work on the philosophy of history by an American philosopher, Hempel, where he was squeezing history into what he called the 'Covering Law' scheme of explanation, and I am going to argue that history can't be squeezed – not simply by pointing out, which is true of course, that the results after the squeezing are not recognisable as history, but by a more *a priori* argument.

The key word which will separate me from the other three is the word 'algorithm'. Waddington with only a very little prodding will produce algorithms in his account of how embryos develop, and Longuet-Higgins believes that his computers can do everything because everything that can be done can be done according to an algorithm, and yesterday Kenny – I quote – said that 'if it is an inference at all it must work in every case'. Now I may be misquoting, or misquoting his intention, but there is here a certain ideal of being able to have a decision procedure, a method, a procedure of deciding whether something is true or false which will apply in every case. This is true of the sciences, but it is very typically *not* true of the humanities. We don't think that we can decide whether, if Hannibal had marched on Rome, Rome would have fallen, by looking for some universal law which applies to all Rome-like cities being marched upon by Hannibaline armies. The importance for our present concerns is whether we can have every decision being able to be decided by some decision procedure, whether every problem can be decided by an algorithm.

Some of you have already indicated to me that they rather hoped that I was going to prove Gödel's theorem. I am not going to do that, partly because it is very difficult, but more because it is exceedingly dull and takes about forty-seven pages of close, usually Germanic, print. But I shall explain what to do if you meet a computer one dark night on Forrest Hill. The first thing is to get into conversation. We have our doubts whether computers can talk, but Longuet-Higgins assures us that they can, and it is always a good thing to 'jaw jaw rather than war war'. Engage him in a Socratic dialogue and ask him various questions. First of all, various questions to make sure that he is really a computer and not Longuet-Higgins in disguise. The crucial one is, does he operate algorithmically — that is to say, does he have just simply a certain set of very definite instructions, according to which he will answer any question that you put? If he answers 'yes' to this, then he is a computer, but also then you can start numbering his instructions and any combination of these. There can't be more than $\aleph_0$ (the smallest sort of infinity that there are) instructions according to this principle; and therefore you can number them 1, 2, 3, 4 and so on up to infinity. Having got to this point, you also start to number the problems, the questions you can put to him, and the key to the whole way of dealing with computers is that they both can be numbered and therefore you can start playing off one against the other. And then you start putting more difficult questions. You ask the computer, 'Dear computer, what is your procedure for telling that problem number n cannot be solved by procedure number n?' And if he answers '7,777,777' — supposing he gives this as his answer for his procedure for telling that problem number n cannot be solved by procedure number n, then naturally the next thing to do is to ask him 'Can problem number 7,777,777 be solved by procedure number 7,777,777?' and if he is a very arrogant computer he may say 'yes'. If he says 'yes', then you point out that that procedure is one which tells him that that problem cannot be solved by that procedure. So perhaps he is a more modest computer and will say 'no', and then either you could start niggling and induce him again into an inconsistency or you might be generous and allow his humility at the price of getting him to admit his humanity, and show that here is a problem that he can solve, but not by that procedure.

Now this is a tricky argument; it is a finicky argument; but it is in fact a fair one. It is one of a great range of theorems which have been discovered, ranging from Church's theorem through Gödel's theorem to Tarski's theorem. Church's theorem shows that although a very well-paid and patient computer could go on if it had infinite time and infinite money, proving all the theorems of the predicate calculus, it could not show all the well-formed formulae which were not theorems to be non-theorems. That is one end. In the middle there is Gödel's theorem, which I think is the most interesting one because it has a certain interplay between truth and proveability; and at the far end Tarski's theorem which establishes that within any formal system in which the elementary operations of arithmetic can be formalised, it is impossible to have a predicate which has the typical properties of the word 'true'. That is, truth cannot be formalised in computer language, with the consequence that the computers in their languages, Algol, Fortran, or anything else, have to dispense with the concept of truth. And this seems to me to lead us to a certain creative theory of truth, something different from the traditional theories which are normally given — the correspondence theory and the coherence theory and the ditto theory of Strawson in his earlier years. I am not very clear exactly how this is to be worked out. What I think we do see is that if we are to give an adequate characterisation of the intellectual powers of man, then when we are concerned with what things are true, we cannot hope to be able to reduce them entirely to some set of decision-procedures — the set of algorithms which are what computers can do, and what the whole programme of formalism would require that all mental activities should be able to be reduced to.

I want now, having made this negative point, to link it up with a more positive point. That is, the negative point I've made is that some of the characteristic activities of the human mind are autonomous in the sense of not being reducible to, or representable by, purely formal logical or mathematical operations. The positive point that I want to make is certain intimations we have, most typically in moral philosophy, but extending over the whole range of our intellectual activities, about each person being in some way his own originator, his own creator of values. And here I'm going to be running against, I think, a view which is very commonly held, one which certainly goes back to Kant, a view which makes a great separation between moral philosophy and all other intellectual activities. The pure reason is thought of as being something purely academic and to be distinguished from the practical reason; and it is only the practical reason that people need really worry about. Now I want to say not this, but that all our thinking is of a piece and that what holds for our thinking about moral problems holds for our thinking about intellectual problems and *vice versa*. There are of course differences between different disciplines, but there is no big gulf between the one and the other.

I think the reason why people have been much more concerned with autonomy in moral philosophy is that we are all, all the time, taking moral decisions, whereas we are only some of the time and rather occasionally trying to be creative in the mathematical or the philosophical or the other intellectual sciences. Nevertheless, one can see the force of criticism even in the intellectual sciences. After all, though we are sometimes told that computers can compose symphonies, the idea of algorithmic art does seem to be one deeply counter-intuitive, and it is a criticism we often make of people, and we don't need to go to computers; we can often find writers and artists who act entirely according to the rule book, and the results they produce are very wooden. Nevertheless, it is mostly in moral philosophy that we are aware of the importance of autonomy. At the present, we will hear young men talking about the need to be authentic. They complain that their elders, (if they know French) are suffering from *'mauvaise foi'*. Or we can see exactly the same criticism being made of the Judaism of Our Lord's time. Here there was the nearest thing you could have to a moral algorithm. The Scribes and Pharisees had worked out to a very very great degree of complexity exactly how far one could go on the seventh day, exactly what one should do if one's family duties had been pre-empted by some religious obligation. Every possible question had been asked and had been answered, and there was a definitive ruling. Yet, this only produced whited sepulchres who were inwardly ravening wolves. The letter killeth, the spirit maketh alive. It is a lesson that is constantly being re-learnt and constantly being forgotten. It was the same point as was being made at the Reformation. Luther suddenly realises that monkery, going through all the hoops, is just not relevant. This is what he was saying when he was saying that justification must be by faith alone – *sola fide*. But within three or four generations protestantism had forgotten this lesson and had descended into what I might term the Deuteronomy of the will.

It is very easy to sense the importance of autonomy in giving an adequate characterisation of the nature of the mind. It is very difficult to give this characterisation at all clearly, and I first want to put on one side two points which are often read out of the doctrine of autonomy and which do not in fact follow. It is often taken, and it seems to be supported by a superficial reading of Kant, that autonomy is opposed to heteronomy, and that if we are to be authentic operators on our own – each man doing his own thing – then it is absolutely necessary that we should never do anything at anyone else's bidding. And I at this point went to put in a plea in praise of heteronomy. I think the best way of putting this across is to point to the virtue of loyalty. If I am loyal to someone, I show my loyalty not by always deciding myself what is the right thing to do, what's the right thing for him to do, what's the right thing for me to do, *vis à vis* him – but rather to be willing to accept his decisions and then going along with him. He may want to do something which I don't terribly want to do. He may even want to do something which I am not quite sure is the best thing to do – nevertheless if I am loyal I go along with him. I accept his right to lay me under obligations. Exactly the same issue turns up in, often not loyalty to a person but loyalty to an institution, where I want, rather going against the current trend, to argue that often it is the mark of loyalty and of responsible citizenship or responsible membership of an institution to be willing to act against one's better judgment. Well, this is one point that I want to clear on one side because it is one which is very often forgotten.

I want to turn now to a second point, which again very often arises, which is to think that since we ought to each make up his own mind what he is going to do, therefore anything goes. The anabaptists at Munster read out this lesson — obviously St Paul had been having trouble with their predecessors in Corinth; and it needs very little experience of the antinomian argument to shoot a person back firmly and squarely in the absolute conviction that not one jot nor one tittle of the moral or the legal law is to be abrogated; or again, I have noticed it often with colleagues who have had the misfortune to have come in contact with revolting students. It is marvellous what a change of mind this induces. And the important thing to see is that they are right in what they affirm; only, they are often wrong in what they forget. That is, it is not the case that the doctrine of autonomy either in morals or in matters of the intellect means that one's deciding it is so makes it so. My believing that something is true does not make it true, and my believing that something is right does not make it right. The issue of whether something is right or wrong is to be decided perhaps by me, not always but often, but it is not one that my decision thereby makes it be what my decision is.

This shows up very clearly, I think, in the intellectual case. I have been arguing that the algorithms don't answer all the questions. We can't reduce all the operations of the human mind to working according to some set of definite decision-procedures; but we should not conclude from that that in those cases where there actually is a decision-procedure, one is, nevertheless, still at liberty to decide something else. My argument against Longuet-Higgins doesn't mean that either the computer or I am at liberty to say that two and two equal five. Rather what is wrong with the doctrine of complete reducibility to decision-procedures is the completeness. We can formalise different parts of logic, and we can formalise some different sorts of legal procedure and insofar as we do it and do it well we are able to set up procedures which will enable us to see what ought to be done or what ought to be believed, but it will never be a complete job. The lesson that we should draw from the incompleteness theorems is not that formalism is always wrong but that, however far we go in laying down formal procedures for deciding different questions, there will always be other questions which will not be decided by this method. We may then be able to produce another method which will do that other problem but then there will be other problems still, which will elude both the first and the revised decision-procedure. What is wrong with the algorithmic approach is partly that it tries to prevent us asking certain questions, partly that it encourages us to ask certain other questions.

To go back to the moral case. What was wrong with the Judaism or any very well-worked-out legalism is that the question 'what shall I do?' is gradually eroded in favour of the question 'what can I get away with?' This is a very proper question for a man to ask his solicitor, not a proper question for a man to ask his confessor or pastor or any counsellor. Or to take the more intellectual case, where I am very largely inclined to blame Descartes, the question 'is it true?' has been replaced by the question 'can I be sure that it is not wrong?'. Descartes, you remember, shut himself up in an airing cupboard and decided to reject all the beliefs of his elders. There is no doctrine so silly, he said, but that there has been a philosopher who has proclaimed it; and so he resolved not to accept anything other than those doctrines which he could be absolutely certain were not wrong. And this is what a decision-procedure is enabling us to do. We can do it either in the privacy of our airing cupboards or perhaps better in company with other people. Socrates arguing with Thrasymachus, or a man now trying to argue with a computer, trying to see what he can force the computer to accept. This idea of forcing, in Latin *cogo, cogent* – the idea of a cogent argument is a very important question. But it is not the only question. And I think it has been a great corruption of the academic world that too many academics have come to think that this was the important question. It doesn't matter, says one don, that we haven't said very much: at least it can't be wrong. And I want to say that this runs against a certain intuition we have of autonomy, that of each mind being an object on its own, guided by some idea of truth, an idea that is not subjective, not arbitrary but also not entirely external. We can't, and here I part company with Plato, entirely externalise the truth, and think of it as something set out independently of us, timeless, spaceless, and altogether impersonal. If we say this, then we are running against the intimation that we have that truth is something which has to be discovered by us, but is also something which is not made by us. It is something to which we aspire. Well, these doctrines are ones which I still find very difficult to articulate, but they seem to me to be something which is bound up with the concept of autonomy and unless we are prepared to think about 'truth' and about 'argument' and about 'inference' on these lines we cannot really be doing justice to a view of the world which takes seriously the existence of the mind.

Discussion

LONGUET-HIGGINS

Well, I don't know quite where to begin, but I think I would like to start with that dark alley in Forrest Hill where John Lucas has described himself going up and meeting an unknown creature with a great black cloth over it, and trying to decide whether it is a computer or a human being. May I invite you to consider a corresponding situation where I walk up the alley in Forrest Hill, and meet somebody who is in fact John Lucas behind this black cloth, and I try to discover whether he is a computer or a human being. And to do that I address to him the following question, which I shall write on the blackboard. Let me make sure I spell it out right.

'Would a rational being fail to give an affirmative answer to the question on the blackboard?'

You must imagine that I am holding up a blackboard with this writing on it. Now let us just consider the situation in which this anonymous gentleman finds himself. He might give an affirmative answer: he might say 'yes'. But if he does so, he shows that he is not a rational being, because saying 'yes' to this question implies that one thinks that it is rational not to give an affirmative answer to this question. So he has the option either of holding his peace or of changing the subject, in either case of course he fails to give an affirmative answer to the question at issue. And so we conclude that if he is a rational being — that is what rational beings do, they fail to give an affirmative answer — but he cannot say so: so, if he claims to be a rational being he in fact cannot with consistency answer that question. He is in no better position in fact than those poor machines upon which he pours such scorn and I want to ask John Lucas that question.

LUCAS

What was the question?

LONGUET-HIGGINS

He has failed to give an affirmative answer.

LUCAS

This was a difficulty I long ago came across in trying to catch philosophical positions by their own necks, and seeing what it was that was wrong about them; it seemed that unless you had already said what it was, you did not know what it was you were questioning. And the answer to Longuet-Higgins' attack is to point out that he has not asked a question, because what he is referring to is something which is not yet complete, until he has said what the question is. I must know if I am expected to answer, which question . . . and I invited him at each stage to say 'I am very sorry, oh Computer, I do not understand these things very well. Could you say which question?' and then he might put it, namely . . . Back he goes to here. Then having got to there, we have to start off again, round again. Now this is an admirable procedure if one meets a fierce

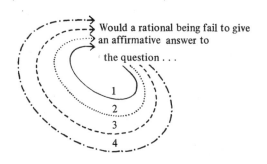

Would a rational being fail to give an affirmative answer to the question . . .

1
2
3
4

Christopher Longuet-Higgins on a dark night, but it does not exert any force against me. What I've got to show, though, is not that I can get away from Longuet-Higgins, but the same technique cannot be used by a computer to get away from me. This is the force of your question really.

LONGUET-HIGGINS

Well, I am saying that you are under the same difficulty as a computer. The sentence on the blackboard is a translation into question form, if you like, of the Gödel sentence to which we give a metamathematical interpretation although it is in fact a statement about numbers. It is the fact that *you* give the Gödel sentence an interpretation which makes it a question which the machine can't answer. It is the fact that I give this question an interpretation, or you give it an interpretation, that makes it a question which you can't answer. But if nobody gave it an interpretation then there would be no question which the machine couldn't answer and so the unanswerability of such questions depends upon them being recognised as questions. But in that respect you are in no better a state than a computer.

Now can I come back and ask you another question which I would like to raise. I think your argument, although you did not say so in quite so many words, rather takes it for granted that we can always see that there is this Gödel sentence and that it is true. Now this depends, I am assured by my better informed colleagues, upon seeing that the axioms are consistent. Now I think it is quite clear that given any arithmetic system we can't *necessarily* see that its axioms are consistent. For example, we don't know whether the ordinary axioms of arithmetic, with Fermat's theorem conjoined to them, are consistent or not. And it is simply not true to say that human beings are always in a position to find and to see the truth of a Gödel sentence.

LUCAS

Can I just first of all continue the first part of the argument. That is about this question, because I feel I do need to answer Longuet-Higgins slightly more fully. The crucial point is one which I have to feed in rather carefully, and that is why I brought in that awkward business about the smallest infinity that there is. The way that we can get round the difficulty of the question, namely is it rational to be able to give an affirmative answer to the question, namely . . . and then going round in a circle is because we can code both the questions and the algorithms of the computer onto the natural numbers.

LONGUET-HIGGINS

But I have coded this onto the blackboard and the blackboard is the address of this question. What is wrong with having a blackboard as an address. Why do we have to have one of the natural numbers as an address?

LUCAS

Essentially because on the blackboard you would never get to the end of your sentence if you were to spell it out fully.

LONGUET-HIGGINS

On the contrary, you can read it right to the end, and so can I.

LUCAS

Yes, but it fails in its reference.

LONGUET-HIGGINS

It doesn't. It's perfectly clear.

WADDINGTON

I think I'll come in on a very different tack. You made some contrasts between the humanities and the sciences. The humanities deal with questions which are eternal questions, to which you can never give a clear-cut answer. For the sciences, you quoted Aristotle or Plato — that you can always tell whether a thing is made of lead or of silver, and you can settle this quite definitely and decide it; and that you gave as your paradigm of science. I think this is unfair — scientific questions are as eternal as those in the humanities are. We are still debating about the nature of the physical world. What happens is that for a time we have a theory about it, and during that time a whole lot of very dull science goes on, using that particular system — measuring this and measuring that, and what have you. But then after a time some absolutely new idea eventually boils up somewhere, a novel idea like relativity which changes the whole idea of material particles and their interactions. These are complete changes of scene, and changes of a whole set of algorithms. During a stable period, when people are all operating within the terms of Newtonian physics, you might say that you could program computers to carry out all these calculations by a set of algorithms. But if you suddenly had to make them work in terms of quantum mechanics you'd have to write a new set of programs. There is a great deal of humanities which is boring as a lot of sciences and that is saying quite a lot. You go away and read a lot of eighteenth century sermons, I don't think you will necessarily conclude that the whole of humanities deals with really intellectually exciting material. The point I want to make, referring back to this discussion of algorithms and computers that I am not a bit expert on, is that it may well be true, as you suggest, that there is always an incompleteness in any given system of algorithms, and I think there is always incompleteness in any given scientific theory. What has to happen then is that a new insight is brought forward and gets embodied in a new, more comprehensive set of algorithms, and you get a new type of scientific theory being employed. Where does this novelty come from? You spoke of it as a creative product of the autonomous individual, and that's one way of putting it, of course. Some people, possibly Freud, have tried to explain this creativity by references to internal mental events. These explanations don't by any means convince everybody, but I think one ought to try to go further than merely saying that a human being has an autonomous creativity. O.K., I think he has, but can we say anything about it?

LUCAS

I concur with most of what Waddington says. My account of the Senate of another university was not meant to be running down the sciences, or for that matter running down the humanities, but merely to bring up a point about different ways of arguing, different ideas of what constitutes a good reason or what constitutes an explanation. It is true, exactly as you said, that one keeps on having new insights in different sorts of sciences – then one formalises it, and then one produces an algorithm sometimes, although not as often as people think, and this is the way that science develops. All I have been trying to do is to give an *a priori* reason for saying that this must be so and that anyone who has an *a priori* argument trying to fit all the sciences into a certain strait-jacket can be seen *ab initio* to be wrong. I think I otherwise agree with you.

KENNY

I don't want to pick a quarrel with John Lucas about algorithms. He lined me up at the beginning of his paper as a great believer in algorithms because I said last night that if something was a logical law it admitted of no exceptions. I continue to believe that if something is a logical law it admits of no exceptions and I am very surprised that John should wish to deny this. Perhaps he does not. What I think he attributed to me last night was saying that if an argument worked in one case it must work in all parallel cases. That also I believe to be true, but of course the discovery of an argument for something is different from the discovery of an algorithm, and unfortunately we don't have algorithms for the discovery of arguments, although we may have for the testing of arguments. In some cases we do and sometimes not.

I would like to point to a limitation on the conclusion of John Lucas's arguments against the autonomy of computers which may not have been apparent. It is essential to his notion of a computer, and indeed, of course to any very strict notion of a computer, that it should work algorithmically. But I think nothing follows from what he said about the possibility of having an autonomous agent that worked electronically. The plain man's idea of a computer is not by John's argument ruled out from someday having the possibility of engaging in dialogue with human beings. Indeed I think that we have no absolutely good reason to believe that it might not be possible to have artifacts which were rational beings. It is only by testimony and induction that we know that we are ourselves not artifacts. It seems to me that though it would be very unlikely there would be nothing absolutely inconceivable in the idea that there might be a knock on my study door one day by a man saying 'I've come from IBM to service you', and then he opens me up inside and shows me all sorts of valves and things that I had no idea were there.

The second point that I want to make about John Lucas' paper concerns the relation between the first and second part of his paper. The first part, you will remember, was devoted principally to logical considerations and the second part to moral considerations. Now I agree with John that Kant made too sharp a distinction between logic and moral philosophy. I think that there isn't an absolute distinction between other areas of philosophy and moral philosophy. I think that results in logic can be relevant to moral philosophy but I don't think that the results of logic which John mentioned were relevant to his moral conclusions. He expressed among other things a dislike of pharisaism. He may be right in his dislike of pharisaism but I don't see how Gödel's theorem or Tarski's theorem has got anything to do with pharisaism unless he suggests that the reason why the pharisees of Jesus' time behaved as they did was that secretly they were computers working on algorithms. I don't think that one can use Church's theorem to lead one into the church quite so quickly.

LUCAS

Can I start by apologising to Kenny that I maligned him about the laws of logic. I think if there is a difference between us it is infinitesimal, and I am glad to welcome him on my side. On the second point that he has made and the main point of Longuet-Higgins I feel some hesitation. I want to argue here but it is something that I have already done in print. I think I shall just allow myself a few words briefly on the possibility of a person being made of electronic hardware. The argument that I have been putting forward is entirely a logical one and has got nothing to do with the hardware. And Kenny is absolutely right to say that my arguments won't tell me what that animal is — that I meet on Forrest Hill — is made of. He might be made of DNA or he might be made of selenium cells. I can't tell. All I can tell is the principles according to which he is made, and although the IBM man might come and open me up, what he can't do is to service me in the ordinary standard sence because this would mean that he was going to put in the right algorithms, he knew exactly what I should be doing, and this is what the incompleteness arguments will tell against. That is to say, although it is a matter of empirical fact true that all the embodiments of minds that we meet on the face of the earth are born of women and begotten in the normal course of events, this is not a conceptual truth and it could be that there was as it were a very complicated thing with lots.of wheels and wires which got beyond the capacity of any man to control, not simply as a matter of complexity but rather that it started having, as we might say, a mind of its own. That is to say, it decided things neither according to a random principle nor according to anything we could programme into it but which we could nevertheless recognise as rational.

LONGUET-HIGGINS

I would like to take you up on that because in your book you have in fact argued from the nature of mind to some physical conclusions about determinism, in fact your argument essentially says that because of the nature of mental activity therefore human beings cannot be automata. I reject this assertion. But it seems to me that if you met somebody in Forrest Hill and they seemed to you to be rational you would have to conclude that they were not made of the usual computer hardware because at least ideally, though not in practice, computer hardware is deterministic in its operation. It never of course really is, because things go wrong; but in principle.

LUCAS

I go on the principle of it. That if it is deterministic in its operation that I can get a foothold for my argument; if it does operate algorithmically then the argument will go through. It is true, what Longuet-Higgins pointed out, that in order to establish the truth of Gödel's theorem one needs to assume the consistency of elementary number theory, but again I am not going to regurgitate this now. I think this can be shown to be a proper premise to assume, but it takes several pages of argument to establish that. Can I just take up a point that Waddington made, who through Freud. . . .

WADDINGTON

May I just say something first, because I'd like to put it in another way. It seems to me you are taking as your definition of rationality, as the criterion by which you decide if the thing you meet is a rational being, that it should at some point behave irrationally − that is to say, not following an algorithm. Is not this somewhat paradoxical? What is the distinction you are making between rationality and irrationality?

LUCAS

Well, I certainly deny that rationality is to be equated with

72

following an algorithm. Here I would go over to a Kennyite position – but I shan't maintain it for the moment. I think Freud is a more popular topic. You see, one of the reasons why this century has seen a loss of faith in reason has been the work of Freud. Freud has forced us to recognise that our reasons are not at all what we thought them to be, and this has been as damaging for our self-respect as Darwin's showing that our ancestors were not what we had hoped they were. But the argument won't work. Those parts of Freud's work where he puts forward, as it were, quasi-scientific theories – he talks about surges and pressures and quantities of libido – has got very little value; and Freud as a straightforward scientist isn't the Freud you know of. The Freud you know of is the Freud of the novels and the interpretation of dreams, who is able to give extraordinarily convincing explanations of why people did things. Although on the surface they might have thought they were doing something for the best of motives, after Freud had heard one or two of their dreams and asked a few questions, he was able to reveal some other reason for their action – one which they were not conscious of. But if he was to be successful as a therapist his reasons in the end had to be ones which the patient could recognize as being his real reasons; and so the reason why Freud does not show us not to be capable of reasoning is because he is presupposing the standard form of understanding what are the reasons for actions. It is only because he is presupposing this, that he is then able to show that quite often we have been misleading ourselves about what our real reasons for actions are. That is, he is appealing from one level on the surface of the mind, in which we have one set of reasons, to another level of the mind, where we have another set of reasons; but those other reasons are of the same logical type. They are reasons for action, reasons which we can understand ourselves wanting to act upon, reasons which perhaps are not very reputable ones, but nevertheless rational ones, and not in the least bit the causal concomitances for the purely algorithmic exercises which is the alternative which is being put forward to us. Therefore I go along with Freud. I walk along to the end of the road, and then show that he is in fact an unwilling ally of mind, and not the antagonist that you had supposed.

KENNY

Could I say something about the relationship between being deterministic and being algorithmic? I was arguing last night that something could be deterministic and yet have the properties of mind such as autonomy and freedom of the will, and tonight I wanted to agree with John that something which operated purely algorithmically could not have the properties of mind. But he said that if it works deterministically then it works algorithmically, and I don't see that this follows at all. There could very well be a deterministic system which operated deterministically, that is to say, each state of it was caused by the previous state, and no other alternatives were open, and yet there be no regular procedures or systematic correlations which would amount to an algorithm.

LUCAS

Here I think I almost have to invoke David Hume. A cause which links an antecedent state of the universe with a subsequent state of the universe, but is not a regular one, is one that I find very difficult to understand, if I'm approaching this from the standpoint of the scientist. I think the difficulty may be (and anyhow it's worth bringing out) that the word 'determine' is used in a wide range of senses, and the word 'determinism' often suffers from a certain ambiguity too. That is, *ex post facto* I can very often say why I did something, and I can often give the reasons why I did in terms of some antecedent state of affairs. The reason why I am here now I can explain, and I can explain fairly fully, but that sort of explanation, although it certainly explains and in that sense also can be said to be a cause of my being here, isn't the sort of sense in which we feel that something is carrying us along willy nilly or that the stars in their courses ordained that I shall be here, quite apart from anything that I decided to do. And so I think we need to press the word 'determine' rather carefully. I am using the word 'determine', and 'determinism' in a sense which can be explained in either a Humean or at least in some scientific sense, of some function which will correlate in a regular and universalisable fashion antecedent states of the universe with subsequent states of the universe. This is the sort of determinism which seems to me to preclude freewill. The fact that Tony kindly predicts that I won't start beating my wife tonight is one which I thank him for, but I don't in the least bit feel that it's a threat to my free and responsible action in refraining from it.

74

ANTHONY KENNY

Sixth Lecture. To Mind via Syntax

In the last lecture, John Lucas suggested that considerable light was thrown on the nature of mind by considering a number of results in formal logic. You will have gathered that it is a matter of dispute among logicians and philosophers whether these results have the implications he thinks they have for philosophy of mind. But let us suppose that Lucas is right in this controversy. I think that the non-logician may feel certain rather human misgivings about his approach. It may be that John can show certain things to be true which no machine could prove. It may be that this shows that John Lucas is no machine — but what of the rest of us? After all, comparatively few human beings can follow Gödel's theorems or Church's theorem. Does this mean that we lack the indefinable property which sets minds above machines? I know that John would reply 'Of course not, the Gödelian argument is merely a way of breaking down the extreme claim "all minds are machines": once it has been accepted that some minds are not machines then there is very little reason for thinking that any are.'

Still, there remains something to be said for trying to find a way into the study of mind which travels *via* a less esoteric capacity than the ability to outwit computers by producing their Gödelian formulas. And that's what I hope to explore this evening under the title *'To Mind via Syntax'*. For there is reason to believe that considerable new light can be thrown on the human mind by a study of the skill which everyone in this room shares — indeed which every child in these islands over the age of six shares — the ability to frame and understand English sentences. So I want you to shift the focus of your attention from logic to linguistics, from Gödel to Chomsky.

The early work which brought Chomsky into public notice was predominantly within the specialised area of linguistics. But it has been Chomsky, I think, more than any other linguist, who has drawn the connections between the special-ised area of linguistics and psychology in general. Especially since his famous hostile review of Skinner's *Verbal Behaviour*, Chomsky has stressed the implications of his linguistic work for psychology and philosophy of mind. I am no linguist, and therefore am not competent to evaluate his work in linguistics. Why then do I talk about him at all? I am emboldened by Chomsky's own hostility to the compartmentalisation of disciplines. I think he believes that fundamentally philosophy, psychology, and linguistics are a single discipline, and perhaps he is right.

If we study the phenomena of language-use, Chomsky believes, we are led to postulate for explanatory purposes abstract structures at four levels of abstraction.

First of all, in order to describe the grammatical structure of the sentences produced by native English speakers, we must postulate certain abstract mental patterns which underlie these sentences. These abstract mental patterns are called 'deep structures', by contrast with the surface structures of the audible and visible sentences.

Secondly, in order to explain how a language-user can produce from these deep structures the actual sentences of his language, we must postulate that he has internalised rules for certain grammatical transformations that map deep structures onto surface structures. And in order to explain the production of the deep structures themselves we must postulate that he has internalised rules for their generation. We must postulate that he has internalised a particular generative grammar. So that's the second level of abstract postulate — postulation of a particular grammar internalised within the speaker.

Thirdly, in order to explain how a child can learn language, that is to say, how a child can pick up the particular grammar of its language from the fragmentary linguistic data which are presented to it, we must postulate some innate organising principles of universal grammar which enable it to select a particular grammar as a hypothesis to explain the input data. So that is the third level of abstraction — universal grammar as an innate capacity.

Fourthly, if we take the learning of language as a typical example of the acquisition of knowledge by human beings, we may go on — and Chomsky does go on — to draw certain conclusions about human cognitive capacities in general, and thus to offer a general picture of the human mind as mirrored in language. Chomsky in particular postulates a particular hypothesis-forming ability — or rather a general hypothesis-forming ability — a faculty of abduction, he calls it, using an expression invented by the American philosopher, Charles Sanders Peirce. Now I daresay that to those of you who are not familiar with Chomsky's work these four levels of abstraction are pretty unintelligible, and what I want to do in the first part of my paper is to illustrate from Chomsky's writings what is meant by them.

First of all, deep structures. These are most commonly postulated in order to explain our understanding of ambiguous expressions and sentences. Take this sentence: 'The police were ordered to stop drinking after midnight'. If you reflect on that you realise that it is capable of four different interpretations, not because of the ambiguity of any single word in the sentence but because of different possibilities of analysing it syntactically. Similarly, you can analyse in two different ways a sentence such as, 'She is too old to marry' — is she the subject or the object of the marriage? In order to disambiguate particular occurrences of such sentences, we depend upon context and non-linguistic information of various sorts. But simply to know that they are ambiguous, as we all do, is part of knowing the language. And any adequate grammar has to assign a plurality of syntactic descriptions to such sentences.

A simple example will illustrate Chomsky's method of treatment. Consider the sentence: 'I disapprove of John's drinking'. This can refer either to the fact of John's drinking or to its character. We can resolve the ambiguity in different ways in the two following sentences: 'I disapprove of John's drinking the beer', or 'I disapprove of John's excessive drinking'. It is clear in a case like this, Chomsky says, that grammatical processes are involved. And he suggests that our internalised grammar assigns two different abstract structures to the sentence 'I disapprove of John's drinking'; one of them is related to the structure which underlies 'I disapprove of John's drinking the beer', and the other is related to the structure which underlies 'I disapprove of John's excessive drinking'. But, he says, it is at the level of deep structure that the distinction is represented. It is obliterated by the transformations that map the deep structures on to the surface form (*Language and Mind*, 27).

Again, consider the two following sentences: 'John is eager to please' and 'John is easy to please'. These two sentences have similar surface structures. But corresponding to the first one we have the nominal phrase 'John's eagerness to please', but we can't form, corresponding to the second one, the nominal phrase 'John's easiness to please'. Chomsky postulates that the first one has a deep structure which is close to the surface structure, whereas in the second example the deep structure is far removed. Its deep structure is something like 'For one to please John is easy'. Now Chomsky goes on to postulate, to explain this, that a nominal phrase can be formed which corresponds to a base structure, but not to a surface structure; and he offers a large number of examples to illustrate this. This observation lends support to the assumption that abstract deep structures play a role in the mental representation of sentences. I quote from his paper in *Language and Philosophy*, 'We find that when we study English grammar on the basis of this and related assumptions we are able to characterise quite readily the class of sentences to which there correspond nominal phrases of the sort under discussion. There is no natural way to characterise this class in terms of surface structure, since, as we have seen, sentences that are very similar in surface structure behave quite differently with respect to the formal processes involved in the construction of nominal expressions.' (*Language & Philosophy*, 58-9).

Now we have already, as you may have noticed, moved from the first level to the second, with this postulation that nominalisations are permitted corresponding to deep structure but not to surface structure. This postulate is of course the postulation of a rule and it takes us to the second degree of abstraction. According to Chomsky, a native speaker of a language (each of us) has internalised a system of rules that relate sound to meaning in a particular way. The linguist, Chomsky says, when he constructs a grammar of a language is in effect proposing a hypothesis − a hypothesis concerning the internalised system of the language-user. And the linguist's hypothesis, if it is presented with sufficient explicitness and precision will have certain empirical consequences with regard to the form of utterances and their interpretation by the native speaker. (*Language & Mind*, 23). The rule which I mentioned about nominalisations is a syntactic rule, but of course if a grammar is to relate sound and meaning it must include a lot more than merely syntax. It will have to have a semantic component to attach meaning to deep structure, and it'll have a phonological component to assign a phonetic interpretation to a surface structure − syntax including both the deep and surface structure (*Topics in the Theory of Generative Grammar*, 16). In this evening's lecture I am going to concentrate on syntax, reserving the topic of semantics for tomorrow night when Longuet-Higgins will be dealing with it. So far as I understand, phonology is a topic that we are both going to leave out in the cold.

Now, at the third level one can search for explanatory theories of a deeper sort. A grammar is one level of explanatory theory of linguistic output. The native speaker has acquired a grammar on the basis of very restricted and degenerate evidence − the mouthings and cooings of parents, and so on. The grammar has empirical consequences that extend far beyond the evidence. That is to say, the speaker can understand and invent grammatical sentences that he has never heard. At one level, the phenomena with which the grammar deals are explained by the rules of the grammar itself. At a deeper level these same phenomena are explained by the principles that determine the selection of the grammar on the basis of this evidence. The principles that determine the form of a grammar, and select a grammar of the appropriate form on the basis of certain data constitute a subject that might, following a traditional usage, be termed 'universal grammar' (*Language & Mind*, 24).

So Chomsky postulates in the new-born or almost new-born child knowledge of universal grammar. Of course, the grammar attributed to the child is universal, not particular. We can't attribute knowledge of English to the child as an innate property, because we know that the child can learn Japanese as well as English (*Language & Philosophy*, 62). But we have the situation that a child who initially doesn't have knowledge of a language constructs knowledge of a grammar on the basis of certain data. The input is the data, the output is the child's knowledge of the language, and any scientist trying to study a black-box which had certain data as input and a grammar as output would conclude that any property of the output which went beyond the organisation of the input must in some way or other be attributed to the character of the device. And anything that was to be attributed to the device on the strength of the study of this input/output relation would, according to Chomsky, be a universal of language (*The Listener*, 30/5/68).

Now what would these linguistics universals look like? What sort of thing would they be? Consider a simple example which Chomsky has used several times, namely the rule for forming questions from the corresponding statements. Take the English statement 'The dog in the corner is hungry'. From this we can form the question 'Is the dog in the corner hungry?' Now what is the rule according to which this transformation is carried out? It is by no means easy to state it accurately, but as an approximation we might suggest that the occurrence of 'is' which follows the subject-noun phrase in a sentence of this kind is moved to the beginning of the sentence. Now this rule has a certain feature of great importance. It is what is called 'structure-dependent'. That is, in order to apply the rule you have to consider not merely the sequence of elements that constitute the sentence but also their structure. You have got to be able to recognise a noun phrase for what it is. It would be very easy — mathematically it would be much simpler — to form structure-independent operations. For instance, one very simple structure-independent operation would consist in reversing the sentence and forming the question 'Hungry is corner the in dog the'. This would be mathematically a much simpler thing to operate than the rule we have. A computer could do it much more easily than it could do what we do. Nonetheless, according to Chomsky, all formal operations in any known grammar are structure dependent, and this, as he says, is hard to explain on any grounds simply of utility or biological efficiency. One would expect the mathematically simpler operations to be chosen. So that is the kind of thing that he postulates as a universal of universal grammar, the rule that the rules of particular grammars must be structure-dependent. You can see that what is postulated is something highly abstract.

We can proceed, and as time goes on Chomsky seems to proceed further and further in this direction, to a fourth degree of abstraction. On Chomsky's account, as we have seen, the child's acquisition of knowledge is a kind of theory construction, which proceeds under strict limitations on what is to count as an admissible theory. And this is most readily understood if human theory construction in general is subject to limitations, if man's mind has a natural adaptation to imagining correct theories of certain kinds. The ability to learn language is, according to Chomsky, only one faculty of mind, and there are others. Logical and mathematical powers are quite distinct from the language faculty. The language faculty is the one that constructs the grammar out of the input, but we have many other faculties. Though human children learn languages which have only structure-dependent transformations, it may be that other minds, say Martians if there are any, have languages which have structure-independent transformations, and there is no reason, if we ever met them, why we shouldn't be able to puzzle out what they meant, as a sort of mathematical puzzle, using our mathematical abilities. But if Chomsky is right this would not be as easy as to learn a human language, constructed in the manner which he postulates is specific to the human species. (*The Listener*, 30/5/68).

Now, in postulating universal grammar as an innate structure, Chomsky is explicitly allying himself with a rationalist tradition going back to Descartes, and taking sides against the empiricist tradition, dominant, or certainly dominant until recently, in linguistics and philosophy. Chomsky has also praised Descartes for explicitly recognising something which more sophisticated linguists had ignored — namely, the creative aspect of language use: the distinctively human ability to express new thoughts and to understand entirely new expressions of thought. This creativity has three elements. First of all, language-use is innovative: much of what we say in the course of normal language is entirely new, and not mere repetition of anything we've heard before. One can understand without difficulty an astronomical number of sentences in one's native language, and indeed the use of language is potentially infinite in scope. The normal use of language, though, is not only innovative and potentially infinite in scope, it's also free from the control of detectable stimuli, either external or internal. But despite this, it is appropriate and coherent in a sense which is difficult to make precise, though clearly meaningful since we can distinguish coherent use of language from the ravings of a maniac, or the output of a computer with randomising element. (*Language & Mind* 123).

Chomsky's proposals, which I have summarised, are the subject of hot debate among linguists, psychologists and philosophers. Every step of the argument I have outlined has been challenged, right from the initial postulation of deep structures. Some linguists reject the need to go beyond surface structures, and to postulate the transformations from which transformational grammars take their name. As I've said, I'm not competent to assess the linguistic merits of these proposals. I can't judge whether these four abstract structures he postulates are either necessary or sufficient to explain the linguistic data adduced in evidence for them. As a philosopher, however, one doesn't have to wait for the results of the linguistic research in order to assess some of the consequences of Chomsky's proposals for the philosophy of mind. The philosopher can simply ask 'Suppose that the linguistic facts were to turn out exactly as Chomsky supposes, what consequences would this have for the understanding of the nature of mind? Would it have the consequences Chomsky himself thinks it would have?'

I want to go some way towards answering this question, but before doing so I have to introduce one more theoretical distinction. Chomsky distinguishes between what the speaker of a language knows implicitly, which he calls his *competence*, and what he actually does with his knowledge, his *performance*. He says a grammar in the traditional view is an account of a competence. It describes, attempts to account for, the ability of the speaker to understand an arbitrary sentence of his language and to produce an appropriate sentence on a given occasion. Performance provides evidence for competence, and competence provides a partial explanation for performance. But to explain performance fully, one needs much more than an understanding of competence. One must take into account a number of contingent factors, things like the shortness of memory span, variations of attention, changes of mind in mid-sentence, and so on – things which would make it impossible to predict a person's performance from even an exhaustive knowledge of his competence (*Topics in Generative Grammar*, 9).

Now, armed with this distinction, let us consider a very minor linguistic skill – something which is only a minute fraction of our competence. I refer to the ability to construct the names of the natural numbers: the ability, if you like, to count. This example is suggested by a letter of Descartes, which is one of that philosopher's fuller statements about the nature of language. In 1629, Father Mersenne posted to Descartes a proposal by an un-named author for a universal grammar with an international lexicon, and Descartes sent back several pages of destructive criticism. At the end he went on to say

'I believe that it would be possible to devise a system to enable one to make up the primitive words and their symbols in such a language so that it could be learnt very quickly. Order is what is needed: all the thoughts which can come into the human mind must be arranged in an order like the natural order of the numbers. In a single day, one can learn to name every one of the infinite series of numbers, and thus to write infinitely many different words

81

in an unknown language. The same could be done for all the other words necessary to express all the other things which fall within the purview of the human mind. If this secret were discovered, I am sure that the language would soon spread throughout the world.'

There seems something utopian in the idea that all the objects of human thought could be ranged in an order comparable to that of the natural numbers, but Descartes was surely right that the ability to name numbers is itself a sufficiently remarkable one. It has many of the properties which Chomsky insists on in language-use. Knowledge of how to name numbers is innovative in the sense that we can all formulate and understand without difficulty, names of numbers which we have never before uttered or heard. Much of our linguistic use of numerals is also remarkably free from stimulus control: it can hardly be seriously suggested that the utterance of a certain number can be explained as a response stimulated by the presence of n perceptible objects, since at every moment of our lives we are presented with numerable objects, objects numerable in countless different and incompatible ways.

The third of the Cartesian criteria for the creativeness of language, the one which was hardest to make precise, was coherence and appropriateness. In the case of the use of numerals we have rather precise criteria of coherence, the rules of arithmetic; and we have extremely generous standards of appropriateness — to count things or to do mental arithmetic is by itself hardly ever a sign of madness. All this is rather striking in view of the fact that by comparison with other linguistic skills the ability to count appears the most mechanical and the least creative. Finally, as Descartes stresses, the ability to count is, paradigmatically, the ability to make infinite use of finite means. So much so, that to this day text books of transformational grammar point to the existence of an infinity of numerals as the best proof that language itself is infinite. On the other hand, the ability to count doesn't raise a number of the more technical linguistic issues which divide Chomsky from other grammarians.

Obviously, the ability to count has a semantic as well as a syntactic element, and that I shall leave to Professor Longuet-Higgins. I believe that he and his associates have done some interesting work on it. I just want to talk about the syntactic element in the knowledge of numerals, namely the ability to detect well-formedness and ill-formedness in numbers. Each of us here knows that of the two following strings the first is well-formed and the second is ill-formed, as the name of a number. 'One million, nine hundred and thirty eight thousand, two hundred and nine' is all right, whereas 'Two hundred and nine, one million, and nine hundred thirty and thousand eight' is not. Probably none of us have ever heard those particular strings before. There is literally no end to the number of such names of numbers that we could form and evaluate — at least, if we allow iteration as in 'a billion billion billion and one'. Clearly, this is quite a remarkable ability, if one reflects on it, and it is one to which Chomsky's distinction between competence and performance clearly applies. When one acquires the competence, one acquires the ability to write infinitely many words. But clearly no-one, as a matter of performance, ever has or ever will write out an infinite set of names of numbers.

One thing that Chomsky stresses about competence is that it isn't necessarily open to introspection. A person is not generally aware of the rules that govern sentence interpretation in a language that he knows. Nor in fact, he says, is there any reason to suppose that the rules can be brought to consciousness, or even necessarily the empirical consequences of these rules. I think Chomsky is right in saying that there is no paradox in the idea that one may know how to apply rules which one cannot formulate and indeed that one may not even realise without special instruction the different ways in which one can apply rules that one does possess. He has quite an interesting illustration of this, in the expression 'I had a book stolen'. When one first hears this, it's hard to detect any ambiguity in it, yet in fact it can be interpreted in three totally different ways. Consider the following extensions: 'I had a book stolen from me last night', which is the natural one; 'I hired a burglar and I had a book stolen for me'; 'I had a book stolen, and half a dozen spoons, but before I could steal the rest of the library the police arrived'.

In the area of counting it isn't easy to illustrate unconsciousness of application of the rules, but the unconsciousness of the rules themselves is patent. We can all of us detect misplaced 'ands' in the formation of numbers in English, but even the most fluent English speaker, without reflection, is hard-put to give the rule for the placement of 'and' or the rule according to which 'ninety-eight' is well-formed and 'eight-ninety' is ill-formed.

When Chomsky distinguishes between competence and performance he appears commonly to have in mind the difference between competence and deficient performance — for instance, the incorrect enunciation of a numeral which is too long to carry easily in the head. But of course there is a difference, a philosophical difference of category, between a capacity and its exercise, which distinguishes a competence from even the most non-deficient performance. It isn't because of defects in the performance of counters that one cannot exhaust the infinity of the capacity to form numbers. And there is a categorial difference between a capacity and its exercise, even when the capacity is one that is exhausted by its performance — for instance, the capacity to commit suicide, if it is ever expressed in performance, is exhausted by a single successful performance. There is also another important categorial difference between a physical structure which exhibits or embodies a capacity, and that capacity itself — for instance, between the structure of a thermostat and the thermostat's ability to regulate the temperature. It seems to me doubtful whether Chomsky pays as much attention as he should to such categorial differences, and the value of his contribution to the understanding of mind may perhaps suffer in consequence.

There are, in Chomsky's writings, three claims of ascending strength, each of them made about each of these structures. The first is that these abstract structures *exist*; the second is that they exist *in the mind*, and the third is that they exist *in the form of knowledge*. And each of these three claims raises different and serious philosophical problems.

With regard to the first one, I think no particular philosophical difficulty arises in postulating deep structures, if these are regarded as processes which occur in time, related to the time in which surface sentences are uttered. I'm not very clear whether Chomsky does think of deep structures as processes in time. On the one hand, he often talks about them as if they were, and it seems that any empirical verification of his theory about them must involve there being processes in time. On the other hand, he insists that the generation of deep structures is a purely formal, descriptive, matter, and he regards it as an imperfection in Cartesian theory of language that the transformational operations relating deep and surface structures are actual mental operations. (*Language & Mind*, 16).

There is, as I say, no particular difficulty if they are processes in time because we do have a fairly clear notion of what is meant by the structure of processes in time. But there seems to be a great difficulty in understanding what is meant by the structure of a competence, if a competence is a capacity and not the physical basis for a capacity. A thermostat has parts which fit together in a certain way, but does its ability to regulate the temperature have parts? It doesn't seem to me at all clear that we can make sense of the notion of the structure of a capacity. When Chomsky does talk about competence and their structures, it is surely more likely that he means the structure of the material basis of the capacity, than a structure of the capacity itself — a sort of black box specification. The reason for talking of a structure of a capacity, such as a competence, rather than of its material basis, is that one might only be able to define the parts of the structure in terms of their function, without having any understanding of the nature of the material embodiment of the structure; just as one might well know that the body, since it regulates its own temperature, must contain a thermostat, and yet have no idea of the material structure of the thermostat.

This procedure is, no doubt, legitimate, given that we know so little of the neurophysiology of language. But notice that if this is a correct interpretation of Chomsky, he is appealing tacitly to the principle that in order to have an output of a certain complexity a structure must itself have at least as much complexity. This may be true, and it may be a good heuristic principle, but it isn't an *a priori* truth and it should be stated explicitly. If this interpretation is correct, why then does Chomsky say that the structures are in the mind, and not say 'in the brain'? One reason, once given in conversation by Chomsky for not saying that the structures are in the brain is that we don't yet know enough to be sure where in the body the physical analogues of the capacities postulated will be located. As an admirer of Chomsky once put it to me, 'For all his theory says about it, they may be in the left foot'. Without going so far as that one might say that for all we know the structures may be embodied in a system of properties still as unsuspected by us as electrical properties were by Descartes, so that our present neuro-physiological guesses will in time look as quaint as Descartes' hydraulic hypotheses.

Now all this may be a good reason for not attributing linguistic abstract entities to the brain, but of course not being in the brain is not by itself a sufficient condition for being *in the mind*. We normally take it as a criterion for something's being in the mind that it's something about which its possessor can answer questions if asked. But this is not the only possible criterion, and I think Chomsky is right to play down the role of introspection. The reason for regarding these structures as mental – the most obvious one – is that they are structures postulated to explain an activity which is surely a mentalistic one, namely language. But this can't be the only reason for attributing such structures to the mind, because if this were all the explanation would be in danger of collapsing into an explanation of the same form as the theory that opium puts people to sleep because it has a dormitive power. The crucial point is surely that these postulates are postulates whose existence is verified by the occurrence of exhibitions of mental capacity – what Chomsky, not altogether happily, calls the 'linguistic intuitions of the native language speaker'. Since the intuitions which are predicted by the theory are not the same phenomena as those which it's called on to explain, the ghost of vacuousness can be exorcised.

Thirdly, and finally, let's consider the postulation that these structures are present *in the form of knowledge*. This seems quite reasonable in the case of deep structures, which can be brought to consciousness by suitable instruction, like the case of the various interpretations of 'I had a book stolen'.

But once we reach the stage of universal grammar, it's hard to see which of the criteria by which knowledge is ascribed to human beings still remain. It's occurred to many philosophers to ask why knowledge of universal grammar should be attributed to children, when knowledge of Kepler's laws is not attributed to planets. Chomsky's standpat reply is that the attribution of knowledge of Kepler's laws doesn't contribute to the explanation of planetary motion; that the attribution of a knowledge of the rules of grammar does contribute to an explanation of the speaker's ability to use a language. But this answer is inadequate, because even if it's been shown that the internalisation of grammar plays a part in the explanation of language-use, it hasn't been shown that any part at all is played by the assumption that the internalisation is present in the form of knowledge, and indeed the content of this claim has not been made clear, though of course the impact on an audience of the idea that a child knows a universal grammar, is usually quite striking. Chomsky's alternative reply, which is one which is likely to reduce the impact, is that whether this is knowledge or not is simply a sterile terminological matter. But this isn't so. On Chomsky's own account, knowledge of language differs from other forms of knowledge in that by definition a man cannot be wrong about his own language. Now if this is so, then this must make us hesitate not only whether to apply the word 'knowledge' to this, which is, as Chomsky says, comparatively trivial, but much more it must make us hesitate to use a man's grasp of his grammar as a paradigm for the understanding of human cognitive ability in general, which is what Chomsky does in moving from the third to the fourth degree of abstraction.

To sum up. Chomsky has three theses about these four abstract structures. From a philosophical point of view, it seems to me that as the theses get stronger, and as the abstractions get more abstract, the problems not only of verification but actually of content become more and more serious. The parallel with Freud is inescapable and is indeed invited by Chomsky himself. Freud's postulation of an unconscious structure of affection, of volition, is at its most comprehensible and plausible in the case of Freudian slips, where the unconscious motivation is capable of being revealed to normal consciousness by non-theory-laden procedures. Similarly, Chomsky's postulation of an unconscious intellectual structure is at its most comprehensible and plausible in the case of deep structures when it can be revealed by the striking pedagogic devices which Chomsky uses without demanding any commitment to theory in the listener. But as the level becomes deeper, in terms of the theory, and therefore more profound in importance, it becomes, it seems to me, more and more open to philosophical question. If my argument has been right, Chomsky's theories are philosophically most unobjectionable at the point at which they are linguistically most controverted — in particular, on the point in which transformational grammars differ from others. This is, perhaps, not an unexpected result, but I would be interested to know whether a linguist, starting the discussion of Chomsky from the other end, would perhaps come to the same conclusion.

Discussion

LONGUET-HIGGINS

Well, I must say that I agree with all the presuppositions which lie behind Kenny's brilliant analysis of Chomsky's philosophy. In particular, with the view that language is one of the central keys to the study of the mind. But there are three questions I'd like to take up with him. They are quite minor questions.

I'm wondering if he has been quite fair to Chomsky in discussing the concept of competence. If one puts the words 'the structure of a competence' together, one certainly gets something which looks very strange. But I haven't ever seen that phrase in Chomsky's writings: I don't know whether you have? I always understood that the concept of competence was adduced really for the purpose of defining what a language is. And it could be argued that competence is something that might be judged by an examiner, for example, who was reading a student's answer to a question in an examination paper on Logic, to see whether the student had in fact produced a formally correct proof of a proposition which was supposed to be proved, using all the right rules. And I invite your comments on that. The question of how students actually do set about constructing proofs when they are answering examination papers is of course a different question entirely from the question of whether the proof is correct once constructed.

Well now, a second point. You were talking about the naming of the integers, and indeed I think it's a very interesting subject and we have thought about it, as you know. You mentioned that it exhibited the feature which Chomsky called 'creativity' in that people can name new numbers without being stimulated to do so in any obvious way, and certainly that's true. But if I say 'one hundred and twenty three' I say 'one hundred and twenty three' on the basis of a number which I have in mind, possibly in visual form. I may have in mind a row of three digits, 123, and read it off as 'one hundred and twenty three'. If one is not careful one can seem to be suggesting that creativity in language is saying things for no reason whatever, and I would wish to put a large question mark against that, although I'm sure that's not what you meant. And indeed, the whole question of saying what we mean, which I shall be trying to take up tomorrow, is very relevant here.

And thirdly, an empirical question – I don't know what Chomsky's view on this would be. Perhaps you have read enough of his writings to be able to answer. The acquisition of language is, of course, one of the most extraordinary and remarkable tasks that human beings ever perform. And the question is, what conditions are really necessary for the acquisition of a language? If one reads Chomsky one sometimes gets the impression – at least I do – that it is thought to be possible for a child to learn a language by simply receiving samples of that language in sufficient numbers. Now of course our lives and our experience as children are very rich and almost all our experience is non-linguistic. I wonder if you have any comments as to what Chomsky's philosophy might seem to imply about that?

KENNY

Briefly, I think that Chomsky is committed to the notion that competences have structures, in that he thinks of a universal grammar as a competence, and a universal grammar as an innate structure of the mind. He says both of these things several times. And by simple logic it seems to follow that there are competences which have structures.

With regard to your point about creativity, I don't agree that in order to enunciate the name of a number, one first of all has to conjure it up in the mind in arabic numerals and read it off. But even if one has to, this seems to me merely to put the creativity one stage back in the conjuring it up. Though there are differences between the way in which arabic numerals are linguistic, and the way in which the actual English words are linguistic, I think with regard to creativity there is no important difference. The fact that one can make up long numerals, and read long numerals that one hasn't before met is, in the sense in which Chomsky defines, creative. Now this may be taken two ways: as showing that perhaps creativity as defined by Chomsky is not such an exciting thing after all; or, in the way in which I wanted to take it, as showing that just the ability to count is itself something rather striking.

With regard to the third point, I think Chomsky doesn't want to deny that non-linguistic experience is very important in the learning of language. He thinks that linguistic data, non-linguistic experience and innate structures are three independent factors which interrelate together to produce, as an output, the grammar of a language. He thinks that non-linguistic experience plus linguistic data alone, without the innate capacities, would not be enough to explain the output.

LUCAS

I am not going to say anything very polemical now, but I want to draw out one point about Chomsky. The key word is the word 'abduction' on the bottom of the blackboard, which I think is important from the philosopher's point of view, and is important in showing why Chomsky is of philosophical interest: a point which I've always found very difficult. I went to some lectures he gave in Oxford. Enormous crowds of people listening to rather repetitive attacks on Professor Quine, and at last I got what it was, what the mixture was that gave this charisma; it was a mixture of extreme Left Wing politics, and extreme Right Wing metaphysics. And the Right Wing metaphysics, about which he has absolute honesty, he's pro-Descartes, down with Locke: Locke's theory of innate ideas is all wrong. Nevertheless, he conceals a certain ambiguity. You could take it, as I think Chomsky himself takes it, and as his followers take it, that this is a piece of work in the rationalist tradition. We show the limitations of empiricism, and in Chomsky's latest book, which Kenny lent me on the 'plane this morning, he was working it out as an attack on Nelson Goodman's extreme empiricist reconstruction of induction. And the message that comes over here, then, is that there is more to the human mind than can be reduced to any little formula. This is a message which I find very congenial, but it is one that could be taken a different way, and was taken a different way, for instance by David Hume. Hume also came to the conclusion that the workings of the human mind couldn't be rationally reconstructed according to the principles which he took as being essential for satisfactory reconstruction of the human mind. Sometimes he will have it that you can't even give a rational justification of induction. We don't talk about 'induction' any more, but something rather grander, 'abduction'. On other occasions, Hume will allow induction, but then comes to the conclusion that our moral reasonings are ones which are not really reasons at all, but only are a matter of sentiment, a question too nice for the operation of human reason. We have to settle it by our sentiment or our emotion. And the problem which I think now comes to be decided, on philosophical evidence, is whether, supposing Chomsky is right about our linguistic abilities, is this something which is only for Waddington to be interested in. Curious things, human beings: not only are they featherless bipeds, but they've got deep structure, universal grammar. This is a matter of great interest, but only to the biologists who find it very interesting why human beings come this way rather than the other. Or, is it, as once Chomsky, I think Kenny, and certainly Lucas, want to maintain, this shows something very important about human beings. Not merely featherless bipeds, but rational agents.

WADDINGTON

I've got very few remarks to make in this connection, because of course, as a biologist I'm mainly concerned with organisms which do not indulge in language, and some of them have what I should be willing to call 'minds'. They can learn, they can do a variety of performances, but they don't actually talk. However, we'll come back to that consideration later. I've never really felt I had any firm understanding of the Chomsky scheme, certainly when you get down to the level of universal grammar. But I just want to ask a question. We've had this talk about naming, for instance forming correctly formed names of integers. What is the grammar like in languages that don't have, for instance, a zero? Recently I came across some South Africans, in whose native language you can count up only to five; then it is 'many', and no distinction amongst the many. And no zero; The absence of zero, I should think, would make a very considerable difference to all grammatical structures. Is this part of a universal grammar, and does the universal grammar contain a zero or not? Related to this is the question 'Is the universal grammar related to the experienced world?' Chomsky says it's now innate, but I'm an evolutionist, and things become innate through processes of evolution, usually because they are in some way useful. Is this what is supposed to be the case with universal grammars? And if so, what produces a zero in a universal grammar that for a long time lacked a zero? We are told that it was invented by the Indians — a Sanskrit invention, I believe. But how does it come to be invented? What is the status of invention of new items in universal grammar?

KENNY

I think Lucas has wrongly claimed Chomsky as an ally in thinking that the innateness of universal grammar is something which marks human beings off as rational agents. Chomsky believes, I think, that there could be perfectly rational Martians who didn't have our universal grammar innate and for all I know had no universal grammar innate, but learnt language as we learn mathematics. (I'm not quite sure why Chomsky excludes mathematics from depending on an innate component, as he appears to do.) But the Martians, so far as I can tell from Chomsky's brief descriptions of them, could very well turn out to be people about whom all the theses of B. F. Skinner were true, and therefore, from Chomsky's point of view, turn out to be very unpleasant creatures indeed.

To turn from the Martians to the non-human terrestrial creatures whom Waddington reminds us of — I think that Chomsky has had very little to say about the evolution of language-users from animals who did not have the use of language, though he does have a number of rather caustic remarks about people who think that natural selection is the name of a theory with any content. What lies behind these remarks I do not know. But he has always by-passed this question by saying 'well, the first thing to decide is whether or not it's correct that it's innate; only if it is innate do we have to go back and ask the question when, if ever, did it become innate?'

I would like to clarify something in my paper which I think Waddington and perhaps others misunderstood, which was the function of the example about counting. This wasn't meant to illustrate all of Chomsky's theses, and it was certainly not meant to suggest that Chomsky thought that the English or Arabic system was itself innate. It was meant primarily to illustrate the distinction between performance and competence and what Chomsky meant by creativity in language. In fact, the principles of universal grammar are very much more abstract than the rules for counting. They are such principles as 'grammars must contain only structure-dependent transformations', and so to the question 'is there a zero in universal grammar?', I think the answer is definitely 'no'.

Seventh Lecture. To Mind via Semantics

I want to take up where Kenny left off, because I share his conviction that natural language provides us with an incomparable window into the human mind. Indeed, it was argued by Alan Turing, one of the pioneers of modern computing, that any creature which could pass for a human being in a conversation on a teleprinter, must be regarded as capable of intelligent thought. The only trouble with Turing's test is that a computer programme has already passed it. Here's a dialogue which actually developed between Weizenbaum's programme, *Eliza*, and a salesman who called it up by mistake, thinking he was connected to one of the professors at M.I.T.

Salesman Do you think that I can use the computer this morning?

Computer Why do you ask?

Salesman I might be able to make some additional telecomp sales.

Computer Why aren't you sure?

Salesman My prospective customers have never seen a demonstration of the system.

Computer Does this mean very much to you?

Salesman Of course it does.

Computer You seem very positive about that.

Salesman This is ridiculous.

Computer What do you mean, this is ridiculous?

Salesman Is there any reason why I can't use the computer now?

Computer Tell me more about your prospective customers.

Salesman Please dial me up on 491-1850.

It's not difficult, being wise after the event, to see roughly how the programme works. It's designed to hold on to the conversational initiative at all costs, by changing the subject if necessary, in order to hide its inability to answer the human being's questions. But we react to this explanation of *Eliza's* victory with mixed feelings. Having applauded Weizenbaum's technical ingenuity, and his cynical appreciation of human gullibility, we are left with the conviction that *Eliza* has only passed the Turing test by cheating, and that her responses, though a good deal more to the point than a parrot's, can scarcely be regarded as thoughtful contributions to the conversation.

In this lecture I want to try and put my finger on some of her intellectual deficiencies. Not as one of her detractors, because I regard her creation as a major event in psychology, but because I share Weizenbaum's conviction that the serious attempt to model human conversation is likely to be one of the most fruitful ways of discovering the nature of intelligent thought.

It could be argued that the remarkable progress which has been made by Chomsky and his school in the description of natural utterances has been at least partly due to the decision to attend primarily to the *forms* of utterances, rather than to their content. Only when we have brought to order the things people actually say can we hope to relate what they say to what they mean; at least, this is the faith which seems to have inspired much of the modern work in transformational grammar. In this lecture I shall dare to try and pass beyond the forms of utterances to their *meaning* — to venture on to the treacherous ground of semantics. But before doing so, I would like to revert briefly to a case study which was mentioned by Kenny, in order to bring out the distinction between structure and meaning.

Here I'm going to write on the board a little grammar which generates the English names of the natural numbers from 1 to 999. There's a set of words which we can call $W1$, and these are 'one', 'two', ... , 'nine'. There's another set of words called $W2$, namely 'ten', 'eleven', and so forth, up to 'nineteen'. There's a third set of words called $W3$, namely 'twenty', 'thirty', and so forth up to 'ninety'. We can form composite words, $W4$, by taking a word of type $W3$ and conjoining it, with a hyphen, with a type $W1$ word. We can define a class of words, $W5$, to be any word in the set $W1$ or $W2$ or $W3$ or $W4$. We can define a word string, $W6$, as one which starts with the word $W1$, goes on with the word 'hundred', and then optionally proceeds with the word 'and' followed by a word of type $W5$. And then the name of an integer from 1 to 999 is either a word of type $W5$ or a word of type $W6$. That looks very complicated, and it is rather, but we recognize that it's true. Supposing, for example, I want to form a name. I can choose a word of type $W6$; let's do that by taking a word of type $W1$, say 'two', followed by 'hundred'; and then if I've chosen this option I'll say 'and' followed by a word of type $W5$, which might be, say 'ten'. Well now, that grammar tells us what we are *allowed* to say, if asked to name any number between 1 and 999, but it doesn't tell us *what* to say if we have a particular number in mind. At the very least, we should like to have rules for naming any number presented to us in arabic notation; and conversely, for translating any string of words, such as 'three hundred and nineteen' into a corresponding arabic numeral. The general problem of assigning meanings to utterances or finding an utterance to express a particular meaning is, of course, extremely tricky, because a disembodied idea is a most difficult thing to capture. But we can obtain at least a glimmering of how to assign meaning to utterances by thinking about this very simple example. When someone says 'three hundred and nineteen', how do we know what to write down? In this case, it's quite easy to see. We think of the digit whose name is 'three'; the word 'hundred' tells us to put two noughts after it, and the word 'nineteen' tells us to replace the noughts by the pair of digits named by the word 'nineteen'. Each word in the utterance 'three hundred and nineteen' triggers a process in the mind of the hearer, and the overall result of these processes is the evocation of the arabic numeral 319 in the hearer's mind. In the next few minutes I want to explore the implications of this simple idea.

Broadly speaking, I shall suggest that the meaning of an utterance is nothing more or less than the processes of thought which it is intended to evoke in the mind of the hearer, and that the job of semantics is to elucidate the relation between utterances and the processes which they symbolise. In developing this theme, I shall need the concept of a computation, so perhaps I should just explain that computation is anything that a computer can be made to do, by programming it in a suitable computing language. And a program is, conversely, just a string of symbols which, when you put them into a computer, will result in the performance of a computation — or so one always hopes.

Now, broadly speaking again, logical languages are of two kinds, *indicative* languages and *imperative* languages. An indicative language is a language such as the propositional calculus; an imperative language is the sort of language in which we program computers. In the propositional calculus we encounter formulae of this sort: P, $\sim$P, P & Q, P v Q, P $\supset$ Q, where the letters P and Q are so-called 'atomic' symbols, and the other symbols, '$\sim$', '&' and 'v' are called 'connectives'; and you may also have opening and closing brackets in your formulae. There are rules for deciding whether a formula is 'well-formed' or not, and these rules may be compared with the rules of syntax in the natural language. There are also rules for generating new well-formed formulae from old ones, and an enterprising firm has actually brought out an educational game in which the players are required to produce new formulae in just this way. But the whole point of the calculus resides in its semantics, in the way in which the formulae are to be interpreted. The atomic symbols, P, Q, and so on, are supposed to represent assertions — never mind what, we are not interested — which are either true or false. $\sim$P represents the negation of P, and so it is false if P is true, and true if P is false. The symbol '&' is self-explanatory — P & Q is true if both P and Q are true, but false otherwise. 'P v Q' is false if both P and Q are false, and true otherwise. So you must think of the symbol 'v' as representing 'and/or'. And finally there's the symbol '$\supset$' which is sometimes referred to as 'implies'; but this has to be taken with a grain of salt, because the formula

94

'P ⊃ Q' is true unless Q is false and P is true. In other words the formula 'P ⊃ Q' is true even if P is false. But that is one of the well-known little problems about explaining the propositional calculus to people when you first teach it to them. Now, if one of these formulae – let's consider a more complicated one, namely (P & (P ⊃ Q)) ⊃ Q – turns out to be true whatever truth values we assign to P and Q, it's called a tautology; and if turns out to be false whatever truth values we assign to P and Q, then it's called a contradiction. You see the concept of truth is playing a very central role here.

Now there's a considerable body of theory about the semantic interpretation of indicative languages such as the propositional calculus; but far the most interesting part of this theory is concerned with languages whose domain of discourse, on some interpretation, includes the statements of the language itself. In a natural language such as English, the domain of discourse certainly includes the statements of the language, because we can say 'your statement is false'; but as a result we run into the *Liar Paradox*, 'this statement is false'. It was in fact the Liar Paradox on which Alfred Tarski built his famous theorem about the impossibility of expressing the concept of arithmetical truth within arithmetic itself. But perhaps it is not so very surprising that we should have trouble with the concept of truth when we are discussing our own statements. What actually happens when we first meet the Liar Paradox? We observe that it can be true only if it's false, and false only if it's true. So we go into a loop just like a badly programmed computer – and never emerge with a definite truth-value. If the statement did have a truth value we could obviously never find it, so perhaps we should draw in our horns and allow that there are certain statements to which the concept of truth just doesn't apply. But what about the concept of *meaning*, if the concept of truth fails us in such a simple case?

My colleague, Stephen Isard, and I have been thinking about this problem, and some of the following thoughts are as much his as mine. In ordinary human conversation, we make rather few directly verifiable statements; there's little point in telling people what they could easily verify for themselves. We say things for various reasons, but not by any means always to provide the hearer with factual information. If I ask you to shut the door, and you do so, that is enough to convince me that you have grasped my meaning. But my sentence was in the imperative, not the indicative mood. If I ask you the time you display your grasp of my meaning by saying 'half past five', but this time my sentence was in the interrogative mood. Your answer is, of course, an indicative statement, and I could in principle check its truth by looking at the clock; but I probably cannot see the clock, or I would not have bothered to ask the time in the first place. For these and other reasons we have chosen to view English sentences not as logical formulas like those on the board, with truth values in some interpretation, but as messages which are to be interpreted as sets of instructions to the hearer. On this view a natural language is not to be thought of as an indicative language but as an imperative language analogous to the languages which are used for programming computers. When we want a computer to compute something for us, we have to represent the desired computation as a program, an ordered set of instructions in a computing language. When we want a person to do us a favour we can likewise express our wishes by an utterance, a command, or a question in natural language. The other person may, of course, decide not to meet our request; but that does not alter the meaning of the request any more than the meaning of the computer program is thrown in doubt if, on some particular afternoon, the program doesn't run because of a failure in the power supply.

You may be wondering whether, in giving priority to commands and question, I have forgotten about statements. No, I haven't — but in some ways statements are a little bit more subtle. They seem to arise most naturally as the answers to questions, even if the question is not explicit. Take for example the very simple statement 'I do'. If you ask me whether I like chocolate, I shall reply 'I *do*'. But if you hold up a box of chocolates at a children's party and say 'who likes chocolates?', the answer will be '*I* do'. The difference of intonation in the two cases arise from the difference between the questions to which the statement might be an answer. The present situation, in this room, in which I am holding forth in a sequence of indicative sentences, is a highly artificial one. But even on this occasion I'm hoping that each statement I make may raise a question in your minds to which the following statement will help to supply an answer. It is notoriously difficult to try and teach anyone something in which they are not interested.

The view that English sentences are to be interpreted as instructions to be followed by the hearer, explains quite naturally how a sentence may fail to convey meaning in one situation, even though it is quite intelligible in another. If I turn suddenly to the Principal and say 'Follow that taxi!', he will either say 'What taxi?', or, more likely, lead me gently out of the room. Almost everything we say is riddled with presuppositions, and if the hearer doesn't share them, he is unable to carry out the intended computation. And like a good computing system, with internal checking procedures, he will probably point out why. So any good model of human conversation ought to do the same.

Another feature of English that fits naturally into the computational setting is the fact that sentences, especially fragmentary ones, depend for their interpretation not only on the objective situation but on what has just been said. An obvious example is the single word utterance, 'yes', which would be very difficult if not impossible to represent in a formal, indicative, language, because of Tarski's theorem. But 'yes' is quite easy to symbolise in a computing language. The language POP-2, invented by my colleagues in the Department of Machine Intelligence, allows one to conduct without difficulty the following short conversation:

Is 4 equal to 2 + 2?
Yes.

The conversation goes like this: you type into the computer: $4 = 2 + 2$, and then an = sign and a $>$ sign; and you press the carriage return and the computer types back **1, which means 'yes'. (The asterisks, I might add, are just there to remind you that you didn't type that line yourself.)

In the semantics of indicative languages, as I've tried to explain very briefly, the concept of meaning is bound up with that of truth, and the truth of a statement is determined by examining the truth values of its constituent parts and combining them in a manner determined by the syntax of the statement. The semantics of English, viewed as an imperative language, is rather different. Here, it seems, the concept of meaning is prior to that of truth, the meaning of an utterance being the sequence of mental processes which it is supposed to evoke in the hearer, possibly culminating in an action, if the utterance was a command, or in a reply if the utterance was a question. If the utterance was a statement, there may be no observable response, only a change in the hearer's state of mind. But it is quite futile for the speaker to say anything at all unless he has some idea of the hearer's mental state; otherwise, there is no prospect of influencing the hearer's thought processes in an appropriate manner. The situation is therefore a great deal more complicated than anything which we encounter in mathematical logic. But one very useful idea may be borrowed from Tarskian semantics, namely that of determining the meaning of a sentence by combining the meanings of its constituent parts in accordance with the syntax. If I say 'Please shut the door *and* open the window', I have conjoined two sentences, and thereby indicated that I want you to do both the things mentioned. And if I ask 'Did you understand my last remark?' I am inviting you to recall the last remark that I made and to tell me whether you understood it. It seems likely, indeed, that the sole function of syntax in natural languages is to signify without ambiguity the nature and the precedence of the various steps in the desired computation. That is certainly the function of syntax in a programming language, as every programmer takes for granted.

I started by quoting an actual conversation with Eliza Weizenbaum, and making a few patronising comments about her intellectual limitations. Her strong points are her syntax and her conversational strategy. She is very good at distinguishing statements from questions and commands, at picking out noun phrases — 'Tell me more about *your prospective customers*' — and at transforming between the first person and the second person singular. Her weak point is her semantics: she doesn't understand what is said to her, and she doesn't mean what she says. She doesn't understand, because she treats sentences not as pieces of program to be implemented, but merely as objects to be manipulated. She doesn't mean what she says, because her utterances are either pre-packaged or cleverly thrown together from the raw material supplied by her victim. But she has been an inspiration to other people to do better, and great heights have recently been scaled in a program by Terry Winograd, of MIT. Dr. Winograd will be giving a public lecture about his work in this room on Wednesday week, and so rather than steal his thunder, I shall mention some of our own attempts to express semantic ideas in programmatic form.

One of the first tasks we undertook was to construct a semantics of tense and aspect in English, mainly by the light of nature, though we found that Reichenbach had to some extent anticipated our ideas. The problem was to devise a program which would read an English question and convert it into a set of logical operations. These in turn, these logical operations, would then operate on the information available to the program, and generate an appropriate reply. The available information would be partly factual, of course, but partly also linguistic. Because one of the features of human conversation, as I mentioned before, is the frequent occurrence of fragmentary utterances, which depend for their interpretation on the current tense, the current subject, and the sentences which have just been uttered. We are so accustomed to this that we hardly notice it as a problem. But perhaps you will see what I mean in a minute, when I quote some conversation with one of our own programs.

This program is designed to answer questions about the arrival of guests at a party, and it is supplied in advance with the information that Al, Bob, and Bert, Charlie, David, and Derek, Ed, Fred, and others, arrive in alphabetical order. A non-guest, called Cuthbert, hasn't been invited and isn't coming, and the program knows that. The time of speech was originally set for just before the party, and here is the ensuing conversation. (I want you to notice that some of the questions are very fragmentary.)

Human Will Fred arrive before Harry?

Program Yes.

Human Just before?

Program No.

Human When Fred arrives, will Bob have come, since Cuthbert?

98

Program Cuthbert never will.
Human When Bob arrives, will Harry have come since David?
Program David won't have by then.
And now we move the time of speech up to just after the arrival of Charlie.
Human Has David turned up?
Program No, not yet.
Human Has Cuthbert?
Program No, he never will.
Human Will Bob arrive before Bert?
Program Bert already has.

The program works by first parsing the question in a primitive way, to determine the tense, aspect, subject, and time phrases, if any, and fills any essential gaps by referring to what has been said already. It then interprets the question semantically. If the question turns out to be ill-posed, because the tense is inappropriate, or because of some false presupposition about the timing of events, then the reply has to indicate the fact. And that is just about as far as it goes. I could mention some of the problems which arise when we come to think about sentences involving the words 'may', 'might', 'must', 'can', and so on. We are trying to straighten out our ideas about these, and about other modal expressions, by writing a program with which we can play noughts and crosses, and at the same time discuss the game with the program, in English. But perhaps I'd better use the remaining time to try and draw the threads together.

First, and very emphatically, I am not suggesting that human beings are just like computers, or that computers are just like human beings. But our own mental capacities certainly include the ability to compute, and, what is more, to perform computations beyond the wildest dreams of all but the wildest people. The reason why machines which compute arouse such passions is just because, like the dog standing on its hind legs, they can do it at all. But unlike existing computers, human beings can think up programs for themselves, and natural language is the means whereby we suggest programs to one another. I use the word 'suggest' not because I want to build a wall of agnosticism between science and man, but merely because it would be plain folly to assert that the programs we talk are inevitably and infallibly implemented in the minds of our hearers. Of course they aren't — and for a hundred and one very good reasons. We may speak indistinctly, imprecisely, or unintelligibly, and we shall not be understood aright if we fail to understand the mind of the person we are addressing. Human communication is hair-raisingly unreliable. The wonder is that against such odds we can achieve it at all.

Secondly, in a more positive vein, I am trying to recommend a new fashion in the construction of psychological

99

theories. By and large, theories of the brain and its workings are severely limited, both in form and in subject matter. Insofar as they venture beyond purely descriptive accounts of behaviour, the mathematics which they employ is usually limited to elementary algebra, calculus, and probability theory. But the system to which psychological theories are addressed is by far the most complex computing system in existence. Surely its understanding is going to call for concepts and theories at least as sophisticated as those which are found necessary to describe the workings of man-made computing systems? It is not just a matter of putting the old wine of behavioural psychology into the new bottles of logical notation. We must make the concepts of logic and computation an integral part of psychology, and in particular the psychology of language.

Finally, as you may have noticed, my thesis about language has suffered from a very significant omission, which will ultimately have to be repaired. It is one thing to attempt to interpret human utterances as programs for other human beings, but quite another to explain where and how these programs originate. Chomsky has stressed the difficulty of understanding this creative aspect of our use of language, and we are still very much in the dark as to how to explain it. If the meaning of an utterance or a program is the computation which it is designed to specify, how do we manage to pass from a wish to a thought, and from a thought to its expression in a form in which it is intelligible to other human beings, or to a computer? Even computing languages are only *understood* by computers, not actually *talked* by them, and one of the major challenges of the theory of language is to account for the generation of utterances on the basis of non-linguistic motivations. But it would be dangerous to assume that this problem will never be solved, and if it is we shall almost certainly gain in the process some deep insights into the nature of conscious thought.

Discussion
LUCAS

My first complaint with Professor Longuet-Higgins is on his first page — at the very outset, where he sets the examination that Eliza is to take and pass. He quotes from Turing 'any creature which could pass for a human being in a conversation must be regarded as capable of intelligent thought'. And I want to say that Turing here is completely wrong. This may be a necessary condition, but it's not a sufficient one. It may be a qualifying examination — if Eliza can't even fool a salesman, then she's due for redundancy anyhow — but there's a great deal more to it. The so-called imitation game smells very strongly of the old verification principle, that the meaning of a word is in its method of verification, and that we can tell that something's got a mind because its output is just what we should expect, but I think this is very clearly wrong if we move to the paradigm case, which is one which will be boringly familiar to philosophers, when we consider the problem of how we know whether someone else really is in pain. The standard example is a man with a knife sticking through his vitals, with blood pouring out of him, screaming and groaning, and writhing, and then the philosopher, with a certain air of detachment, wonders whether the person really is having pain sensations or whether we should perhaps rather say that to have pain isn't really to have pain, but to be writhing on the floor screaming, uttering 'I'm in pain', and various other things. And it seems to me very very clear that here is one of the many cases where commonsense is a much better guide than philosophy. It seems to me that if we are to do the philosophy of mind at all, we must not reach the conclusion that other people don't have feelings; and that this is one of many cases where the criteria for applying a word, the examination which people have to pass, although important, is not the same thing as what we say when we say that Eliza has got a mind, or that this person really is in pain.

I think perhaps here I might add a little bit in parentheses, out of time, to defend myself against some remarks that were made yesterday, that I couldn't properly deal with — when it was pointed out that my arguments against Turing machines were of a very grisly, uncongenial kind. But the point is that I was taking on a Turing machine on its own ground. For myself, I reject Turing's thesis, but it is worth making the point that even if we are going to examine the output alone, still there is a test which Eliza fails, and necessarily fails, and my defence of the uncouthness of the lingo I use is that if you are going to tell a computer that it is a blockhead you must do so in a language so artificial that even it can understand what you are saying. Still, that's only by the way.

Now, let me rather than go on with several further quarrels with Longuet-Higgins, and agree with him, but disagreeably. That is, I want to take some points he makes — two points — like truth, and his program (rather than propositional) analysis of human language, but take it rather further than he would like to take it. First of all, on his theory of truth, which I want to introduce now. The biblical theologian, Longuet-Higgins, puting forward a thoroughly biblical theory of truth.

LONGUET-HIGGINS

I didn't put one forward at all.

LUCAS

These (the two asterisks on the blackboard — see p. 97) are really breathings or vowels, but the very truth that he was putting forward was one which he expressed in terms of the word 'yes', or, rather better, the Hebrew 'amen'. That's that. And the reason why he was led to this is instructive. Tarski's theorem shows roughly that we can't simply just take the word 'true' as an adjective, in the technical language you can't have a recursive predicate which will pick out all and only those well-formed formulae which satisfy the normal conditions for being true. And therefore Longuet-Higgins sees that we can't hope to have the propositions on the Day of Judgement going up two by two, p and not-p, to be divided as they were always predestined to be, into sheep on the one hand, and goats on the other. This is what we can't have. But he still wants to maintain — and of course he's entirely right to — a difference between some propositions, those which are true and worthy to be received, and others which are less good. And therefore he's trying to put forward a theory in which what you have to do is to pick out some and vouch for those. The computer will vouch for these propositions individually, and says 'yes, this is the right one'. You'll vouch for it, you say this is the one to be trusted, and it is an interesting peculiarity of English and Ancient Hebrew that in these two languages, and as far as I know, alone, there is a very strong connection between the work of propositional approval 'true', 'amen', or אמן and the word for saying 'I trust', 'this is sure', 'this is reliable'. And this is one point which I think is going to be of very great importance for understanding language, that we have to see it not so much as something which can be put in Algol, but first and foremost as an interchange between two (let me call them for the moment) operators, who are putting forward perhaps suggestions, perhaps questions, perhaps commands, and then evaluating what the other person is saying. And somebody puts forward a remark, and you may agree with it, and then in computerese you go **1, or if you are talking colloquial English 'yes', or to follow Strawson you say 'ditto', or if you were in church you might well say 'amen'. And we should see language, if we are going to try and understand language, much more in these personal terms. Earlier, we considered Descartes, and I'll come back to him later, who took a very solitary view of man, and said *'cogito ergo sum'*. The truth for linguistics is *'loquor ergo es'*: 'I speak, therefore *you* exist, *you* are a person'. Or again, to get it into rather more fashionable jargon, you want to say the conversation presupposes an I—thou relationship, rather than an I—it one.

This raises the second point which Longuet-Higgins was taking up, the large number of questions about what is presupposed in programme exchanges with a computer. I'd put in a slightly different way. I'd put in the form of an unpleasing question, 'What does Longuet-Higgins see in computers that he is so keen on carrying on cosy conversations with them?' And he was beginning, and I think this is an important point, where we are getting some illumination, he was beginning to give the answer. He wanted to stress the imperative mood; instead just simply *saying* things, *telling*. One of the things he wants to use language for is *telling* the computer what to do. Another — again English usage is important — he took the example to see what the time was, *telling* the time, where he said — and I think this is very important — that one of the things is where one person is in a position to *tell* the other something which he is in a position and the other is not in a position, to know. That is the *person* theory of knowledge underlined here, that knowledge is not as universal as would otherwise be too easily assumed.

LONGUET-HIGGINS

Well, first of all, I was simply quoting Turing's test as an interesting and rather thought-provoking suggestion which Turing made, but the whole purpose of my paper, as I'm sure you realise, was to try and get inside and see what further conditions we really have to satisfy before we can say that the system we are addressing is thinking intelligently. Just to take a very simple example, we can discover. by examining a computation specified for a particular computer whether when we ask it to multiply two numbers together it really multiplies them together, or merely looks up the answer in a multiplication table. So we have to enquire into the detailed nature of the processes before we can decide whether the meaning is being captured by the system in question. And that was what I was most anxious to show.

As for my 'theory of truth' — I haven't got a theory of truth, and I'm not offering one. I'm offering a theory of the *meaning* of natural utterances. Incidentally, I can't help picking you up; if *'loquor ergo es'* presupposes that you are speaking to a person, do you, when you program a computer, suppose that you are speaking to a person? I personally wouldn't make such an assumption without any further question, but perhaps you would. As for using language for 'telling computers what to do', I think our audience will have realised that this was a mere parody of what I was trying to say. The purpose of today's exercise was to try and elucidate the nature of language, of our own language as well as any other language that we might meet anywhere. And my thesis is simply that language is a medium by which we communicate to one another, and we communicate to one another by influencing one another's mental processes, and it's the active nature of the process of comprehension which is the thing I was trying to express. And the fact that it is a highly structured activity, which of course is at least as rich in its structure as any of the computer programs we can write. And so I'm not quite sure on what grounds I'm being attacked. I can see that you like to parody, but is there any serious objection in your mind?

KENNY

I'd like to take up what I think was the central, original

suggestion of your paper — namely the definition of meaning. You made the very interesting suggestion that the meaning of an utterance was the process of thought that it's intended to evoke in the mind of the hearer, and that meaning is to be interpreted in terms of commanding, or imperatively, rather than in terms of truth. Now I think that this is a very interesting suggestion, and I share your belief that logicians have concentrated too much on the indicative mood and rather neglected the imperative mood. But I'm not sure quite whether your new definition of meaning will achieve what you want it to do. I don't think that your paper did contain a very clear argument in favour of this definition of meaning; after offering the definition you went on to the fascinating account of how your programmes can talk about noughts and crosses, and play 'Waiting for Cuthbert'. But, this was clearly not meant by you as any sort of argument in favour of your definition of meaning, and I think that the argument that did seem to be offered was this: one cannot define meaning in terms of truth, because of Tarski's work. That is to say, one cannot say that the meaning of a proposition is given by saying in what circumstances it is true, and in what circumstances it's false, because of the danger of generating paradoxes like the liar paradox. So one cannot define meaning in terms of truth conditions. And you suggested that instead we approach meaning through the imperative.

Now, if one is to understand the meaning of an imperative utterance, it seems that one must have some idea of what would count as the fulfilment of an imperative. After all, your computer only knows what your instructions to it mean, in the rather Pickwickian sense in which it does know this, if it can carry them out. If what it did were not a fulfilment of your instructions, if it couldn't obey you, then there would be no grounds at all for saying that it knew what it meant. Now, I think it's clear that if one attempts to give an account of meaning in terms of fulfilment conditions, exactly the same problems arise as in trying to give an account of meaning in terms of truth conditions, because one can very easily construct an imperatival analogue of the liar paradox. One can give the command, 'fail to carry out this command'. And this is just as paradoxical as the liar paradox. What is wrong with the liar paradox is that if you take the statement 'this statement is false' you find that, if it is true, then it's false, and if it's false, then it's true. Equally, with the command 'fail to carry out this command', you find that if it is obeyed it is disobeyed, and if it is disobeyed, it is obeyed. I think that if I had enough formal skill I would have no difficulty in re-writing this in a formal way, in the same way as Tarski has done for truth.

Those of you who aren't accustomed to logical discussion I think are very likely to have a strong feeling that there's some trick or triviality about these examples, such as the Gödel formula that John Lucas has talked about, the liar paradox that Longuet-Higgins has talked about, and this paradox of the unfulfillable command that I have just produced. Don't we all know that these are utterly silly things to say? Nobody would ever say them, so why do we have to take any notice of them in trying to construct a theory of language? If we just don't say such things there won't be any problem. In a way that is true, but this knowledge that we all have that these are silly things to say, is itself something that is absolutely crucial to the understanding of language and it's something which a computer can't have. If we knew how to give a computer the knowledge of what was and what wasn't a silly thing to say, then we would have got enormously far in a task where, as Longuet-Higgins has said, we're only just beginning to scratch the surface.

WADDINGTON

Before Christopher comes back, I should like to add something about the question of defining meaning in terms of commands instead of in terms of statements. To the biologist this is obviously very attractive. It's fairly clear that human speech must have evolved from animal communications, and animal communications are basically in the form of commands. Animals see things in terms of actions to be taken, food to be approached, danger to be run away from, and so on, and their communications with each other are fundamentally in the form of commands rather than descriptive statements of states of affairs. But surely, if one accepts that you've got to start by recognising that the fundamental basis of language is in a command mode; surely, the great feature of human language is just exactly that it allows you to make so much more complicated commands. You are going to state, not just 'danger', but 'I see a snake with a black diamond pattern running down its back', or something like this. You can say this is really an instruction to run away from an adder, but really you are *describing* – the command implies a description of a complex state of affairs.

It's how the human language gets complexified that seems to me to be the real problem. The living world gets much more complex as evolution goes on, and this is I think basically to be understood by pointing out that if you've already got four or five systems – elements, a, b, c, d, e, – an animal can always find a way of making a living by exploiting a relationship between the elements b and c, for example. If you've got rivers with snails in them and men walking into them, you can have a Schistosome parasite that lives part of its life in the snail and part of its life in man, and produces a most unpleasant disease in, what is it, about a third of the world's population, or something of that kind. If you have any system which is already slightly complex, evolution can use this to make a further degree of complexity. I suspect this is what must have happened in human language. Possibly, if you say that every noun is really a programme — a chair is something, defined as being something to be sat on — then what you've got to think of is, in what way are these programmes combined with another to make a more complex entity, like a table set for dinner, which has a table and a number of chairs around it. This seems to me really the important thing about human language, because what it really does for mankind is to make it possible to deal with it in much greater detail and complexity than you can do without it. Its point is its detailedness, not just that its fundamental roots are commands.

LUCAS

I'd just like to pick up one of these things — what do I say if speaking to a computer, in regard to *'loquor ergo es'*. The point is I don't regard speaking to a computer, or saying 'stop' to a toy car, which then stops, as *speaking*. And the crucial reason is one which Kenny mentioned, and that is, with instructing a computer — either it does what it is told or it didn't understand the programme. With a person there is another possibility: it understands perfectly well, but says 'no'; and this, what you had on pp. 104—5 as a possibility is the crucial one, that people have minds of their own, and may understand and yet refuse to obey.

LONGUET-HIGGINS

Well, to take the last point first: yes, I quite agree. But I think there are situations in which the same thing could conceivably happen with a computer. The program 'compiles' perfectly well, and it runs, but there is some fault in the output or something, and the result doesn't come out as you want it. I think one can argue about that kind of detail for a long time.

I must say, I found Tony Kenny's point extremely good. I entirely accept what he says, It's no good trying to define the meaning of an utterance in terms of its actual fulfilment. I think, what I was trying to say was that the meaning of an utterance is the computation which it specifies. Now that computation may or may not terminate. It may or may not actually be performed. But that is what the statement means. And if you say 'fail to carry out this command', or 'disobey me', essentially this is a computation with a loop in it, which could never possibly terminate; and we can see that that is the meaning of the sentence. And I think it is too cowardly, intellectually, to withhold meaning from self-referential statements, or indeed from self-referential commands.

I also entirely agree with Wad about the really tough problem about language from the biologist's point of view, being how on earth did it evolve to its present state of complexity and power. And a corresponding ontogenic problem, how do children acquire their knowledge of language? I suppose, as in many other branches of biology, although he would correct me, I am sure, we might expect that ontogeny would recapitulate phylogeny to a certain extent, although doubtless with very many shortcuts. I suppose it's conceivable that one might hope to throw some light on the evolutionary problem of language by actually studying language acquisition in children, but I speak under serious correction here, and I would just like to know whether you think so.

WADDINGTON

I think: probably.

JOHN LUCAS

Eighth Lecture. Consciousness Without Language

I am going to start this evening by pouring a little cold water on linguistics. The last two lectures have been *To Mind via Syntax* and *To Mind via Semantics*, and I want to raise some doubts. Not that I've got anything against language: I'm a language-user myself, and I have strong trade-union feelings in favour of other people who make their living by talking. But, I do want to raise certain points against it; possibly these are – the views I'm going to shoot down – are not views held by either Kenny or Longuet-Higgins. They may protest that I am either parodying them or knocking down a straw man.

I want to argue first that the concept of consciousness is different from that of using language, and that it is perfectly possible to have somebody being conscious without being able to use language. It might seem that this would be a difficult thesis to establish, because we only know, by and large, what another person is conscious of by talking to him and getting him to tell us. This is true, and this is important, and this makes it very difficult for me to produce a counter-example. But there is one, a rather grisly or horror counter-example which comes up from medical practice. For certain operations, particularly, I think, those to do with the abdomen, it's highly desirable to relax all the muscles, and often the drug curare is used, which is so effective that it induces complete relaxation and paralysis. Also, as you may well know, different people have got different tolerances of anaesthetic, and it is possible for the standard dose not to anaesthetize someone. There are cases of people who have been both paralysed and anaesthetized, where the anaesthetic has not in fact worked, and the operation has been performed on them while they are fully conscious, but unable, because they are completely paralysed, unable to make this fact known. I am assured by medical colleagues that this is a very rare case. One of them said it is the doctor's nightmare that this might happen: I thought the patient would have something to say about that! But another, who in fact himself had been having a course of – I think it's called valium – for another complaint, was able to be much more informative about what is called the boxed-in syndrome, the state of consciousness without the ability to do anything or to communicate anything. And from the fact that this does happen, and certainly is intelligible, it follows that consciousness is something different from language, and it is conceivable to have a person being conscious who cannot use language at that time, and I think by extrapolation we can rationally ascribe consciousness to animals who never can use language.

My second *caveat* about the linguistic approach is one about the focusses of attention. I want to take over here a point which I think is most fully worked out by Michael Polyani, in his Gifford Lectures of about ten years ago, *Personal Knowledge*, where he draws a very illuminating distinction between the focus of attention and matters of which we are subsidiarily aware. And this is particularly important for the philosophy of mind, and for our understanding of language. Normally, we take what a person says, not as being itself the object of our interest, but as being the means whereby we come to know what is our object of interest, namely what the other person is thinking. Normally – not always. There are cases, for instance, classical scholars and people who are trying to programme computers and literary critics, where the prime interest *is* in the language. But still, I want to argue that these are subsidiary cases, and that language as an institution arises because of our normal concern with what the other person is thinking. This of course doesn't apply only to language, it applies to the sort of behaviour which we read of as being indicative of another person's frame of mind. One example of this is that occasionally people have rather distressing facial tics – every now and again they grimace. When we first meet such a person, we are very much put off, because we take this as being a symptom of a sudden stab of toothache or mental anguish. When we come to realise that it is nothing of the sort, we cease to notice it, and very soon become entirely unaware of it. That is to say, we are interested in the facial expression of a person as being indicative of his state of mind, and as soon as we cease to regard it as being indicative of his state of mind, we cease to notice it at all, cease even to be aware of it. This point, I think, can be used within the rather traditional framework, of the problem of other minds, to make it clearer what the relation is between states of mind and states of consciousness on the one hand, and overt behaviour on the other.

Gilbert Ryle, in his book, *The Concept of Mind*, gives a brilliant account of what it is to be conceited or to be vain. A tendency to have one's attention wander when other people are talking; to like to be talking oneself, to be fond of telling other people how well one has done oneself; to have lots of mirrors in one's house, to keep *Who's Who* always open at one's own entry. And he uses this, perhaps fairly – I'm not in *Who's Who*, I might say – to argue that vanity is not a sensation. And I think we can concede this. But the fact that all these very different manifestations are recognisable as being manifestations of the same disposition, whatever it is, makes sense only because we have a certain integrative notion of a person thinking too much about himself. And it's because we have the idea of a man's mental attitude or state of mind that we can

109

pool together all sorts of different manifestations, and understand them as being of the same type.

Well, those are arguments which I want to bring before you. They are some of them fairly well-worn ones, as being things to set against the linguistic approach, not by putting up barriers but by indicating alternative approaches, indicating points which need to be borne in mind; we can allow the non-metaphysical, methodological approach of Longuet-Higgins, but say that there are other methods.

Thus far, I have been somewhat negative, not positively negative, but rather wet-blanketish, and I know that Kenny might very well suggest that I've been hired by Our Dumb Friends' League, to put in a plea for those people who can't speak their own minds. I want now to move to a rather more positive approach, and try and bring out some further notions, which will give us a key to the understanding of mind, and not just simply consciousness – I want to go beyond that, or behind it, for something which will pull together both consciousness and the use of language. I want to say that if we are to understand mind properly we should take as our way in, first and foremost, the concept of *action*, or of *decision*. At the moment you might think that I have been billed to reinstate Descartes, who started with his principle '*cogito ergo sum*': *cogito*, I think; *ergo*, therefore; *sum*, I exist; last week, I tried to chisel behind Professor Longuet-Higgins by offering as a second argument a presupposition of all linguistic language. I argued '*loquor ergo es*'; I speak, therefore *you* are. But now I want to go one stage further back, and say '*ego, ergo ago*': I, therefore I *do*. That is, I want to say that the most fundamental concept we should apply to man is that of being a rational autonomous agent, a doer. And that both the concept of consciousness and that of language-use, although independent, are nevertheless subsidiary to this concept. In saying this I don't want to say that you cannot have a state of inactive consciousness – I have just been arguing the exact reverse of that – nor do I want to say that one cannot use language idly, or else St James would have had no call to tell people to be doers of the word, not hearers only. But rather, I want to try and show that the concept of action, of decision, is one which naturally leads to the other two. To put it very crudely, I shall want to say that consciousness is what arises as the feedback of an agent from his decisions, and that language is the means by which we articulate, assess, and communicate our reasons for action.

The most fundamental form of knowledge for an autonomous being is that he should know what he is going to do. I argued earlier that other people cannot know, they cannot predict, what a person is going to do, with absolute certainty. It is up to me, as an autonomous agent, to decide what I am going to do. Perhaps, to use a linguistic argument, since I'm in

110

the company of linguists, I'd point out that the use of the words 'to have a mind of one's own', or 'to make up one's own mind', is just this: to make a decision about what one is going to do. I want to show, first, how, if we take this as our most fundamental concept, we can see a good many of the ways in which the peculiarities of the concept of consciousness arise. First of all, since there is going to be a difference between the way in which I know what I'm going to do, namely as I decide what I'm going to do, and the way in which other people know what I'm going to do, I'm going to be in some sort of privileged position. I have a sort of knowledge which other people can't have, and this is one of the things which we mean by saying 'I am conscious'. There's a special use of the first person singular, 'I know', which doesn't go over into the second and third person singular or plural. Secondly, I can not only make up my mind what I'm going to do; I can consider what I would do if circumstances had been or were different. I can shut myself up in my stove, and think what I might have been doing if it weren't snowing outside, or if I now were in the sunny south, or if I were now flying over the Alps, or if . . ., or if . . ., or if. . . . That is to say, an autonomous agent is not tied down to the here and now; he can make plans for other eventualities. There is a relative detachment of his thinking from everything else. And this is one of the puzzling features of consciousness. This is one of the tools that Descartes uses very ferociously to cut down all the other concepts to size. 'I feign that I have no body; I imagine that I am not in this place; that there is no world'. Descartes is very fond of using this. I think perhaps almost too fond. Surprisingly for a Frenchman, he has not fully taken to heart the significance of the actuality of the present. I should want to argue that consciousness is in some sense anchored in the present, that to be conscious is necessarily to be conscious *now*. But, although consciousness is anchored in the present, it is not confined to the present. I can imagine myself being in many other situations, past, future, actual, possible. And this 'iffy-ness', this hypotheticality of situations I can envisage myself acting in, is one of the reasons why consciousness, and also language, preserves a very high degree of detachment from the immediate circumstances and the immediate situation in which one finds oneself.

A second point which arises from the concept of autonomy is that there is a certain logical gap between input and output. In our last lecture, last time, Longuet-Higgins was offering us as an analogy of language the programming of a computer, of giving it instructions. And then he said 'but the other person may, of course, decide not to meet our request'. And Kenny picked this up as being a crucial concession. It shows that there is, for human beings, for autonomous agents, in contradistinction to computers and automata, a logical gap between what we tell them to do and whether or not they do it. They will do it if they please. But it's up to them to decide whether they will do it or not. This is why children are taught to say 'please'. This also is why consciousness exists. Each person finds himself with many courses of action, and he's not bound to take any of them. He deliberates between then. He isn't bound to take them in the sense in which determinism is usually posed, and which I have argued against elsewhere; he also isn't bound to act on what seem to be very good reasons. For example, I may have a very good reason for not doing something, namely that it is hurting me to go on walking. My ankle is out of joint. This is a very good reason for not doing it — but I'm not bound to refrain from walking, in order to avoid hurting, for a sufficiently good reason. If it seems good to me, I may decide, pain notwithstanding, to go on. That is to say, in this way also, an autonomous agent may be influenced, but is not determined, by his circumstances. These circumstances are present to his mind. He weighs them, then it's up to him to decide what he is going to do. If we take deciding as the fundamental concept, then we will have to raise the question of the connection between my making a decision and actually carrying it out in overt behaviour. There will be something wrong if we had intentions which never influenced performance.

There are people who, perhaps the day after Hogmanay, decide to do lots of things. But we have a special word for this, to indicate that these are not *real* decisions. That is to say, although it is not logically necessary for a decision to be carried out —— it is possible for a decision to be frustrated, it is possible for a decision to be changed—I changed my mind what I was going to do—and sometimes even for a decision to be forgotten, and for many other weaknesses of will to occur —— nevertheless, there is a conceptual tie between decision and actually carrying out the decision, and unless decisions were by and large carried out, then they wouldn't count as decisions. If you put intention and deciding as the fundamental activity of man, you will see that there is a necessary privacy of intention, coupled with, not a necessary but still a very strongly required, publicity of performance. And I want to argue it as a merit of this approach to the concept of mind that, instead of the highly implausible arguments put forward by Wittgenstein about the impossibility of a private language, and the various behaviourist analyses which have been put forward of sensations and dispositions and pains, there' is an entirely innocuous connection between forming an intention and carrying it out. There would be something wrong if I not only formed my intentions in private but kept them there; if, so to speak, I had many, many intentions which I kept *in pectore*, and never allowed them to be manifested to the public in actual action. Or to take a more traditional way of putting it, the way to hell is paved with good intentions.

112

I said some time ago that I would also try and show why the concept of language-use presupposes that of consciousness, rather than the other way round. And I think the point arises because if we have any sort of language, it must tell people something that they didn't know before. Last week, Longuet-Higgins, when he was comparing language to the programming of a computer, took an exclusively second person attitude to language. He was telling the computer to do this, that, and the other. You *shall* perform this computation ending up with two stars and a 1. I want to add in the first person singular, and say that it's also necessary, and pre-eminently necessary, in a language, to be able to say what *I* shall do. We can see this, for instance, in that very primitive language which we use when we are driving. There are few expressions in driving language for telling other people what to do. Very, very occasionally you see a driver waving somebody on. There is, I believe, one expression which is neither indicative nor imperative. It goes into another mood – but almost all the signs of the Highway Code are announcing an intention.

I take this as a rather weak argument for saying that the announcement of intention is fundamental to the use of language. It explains, I think, why we need to have a language. If I am dealing with autonomous agents, only if they *tell* me what they are going to do, can I know as well as possible what they are going to do. It wouldn't happen in a world in which there were no autonomous agents – then we could calculate what something was going to do, and know this quite independently. But once you have an autonomous agent, someone who can decide himself what he is going to do, make up his own mind, then we need language to make public what was originally and essentially private, his decision on what he would do. Not only is it up to an autonomous agent to decide what to do. But in deciding, he is working out his own goals. I don't want to trespass on this too much, because this is what Waddington is going to talk about tomorrow; it is one of the fundamental characteristics of mind – the ability to select one's own goals. But it is important for my purposes to point out that a rational agent acts for reasons: I act for reasons; they are *my* reasons. Typically, I'm in a situation where there are reasons for doing something, and against doing something, and it rests with me to decide where the weight of argument lies, and to make some of these reasons my reasons, and reject the others. One of the reasons why we need language is not only to tell other people *what* I am going to do, but *why* I'm going to do it. I have to show them what my reasons are; and I suggest that a great deal of the problem which philosophers deal with, when they are concerned with states of mind and sensations, and emotions, would be much better approached, and much more clearly understood, if they were seen instead as the communication of possible reasons for action. Most

113

obviously, I think, the concept of pain should be seen not as a sort of sensation but as a very obvious reason for not doing things. It is, as Aristotle would have called it, a φευκτόν, something to be avoided. Reasons apply not only to me; I also address reasons to you. Again, this goes back to the 'please' argument. It is not enough to tell a person what he *shall* do: he has a mind of his own, and he may very well *not* do it. I need rather to give him reasons why he *should* do this, and again these are points which I hope he will become conscious of, and take into consideration himself, and allow himself to be guided by them.

I want, finally, to pick on one other facet of consciousness, which I think also arises from autonomy, and which we haven't yet discussed very much. This is the reflectiveness, and power of self-assessment or of being self-critical, which is characteristic of a conscious being. We feel that to be conscious is necessarily to be conscious that 'I am' – *cogito ergo sum* – is also to be conscious that I am conscious – *cognito me cogitare*. And also to be conscious that I am conscious that I am conscious. And so on. And this is because I am not only able to be detached from my circumstances and envisage that I might have been in other circumstances, and acting in a different situation, but also I can be detached from myself. I can consider that I might have been other than I am, to the extent that I might have already decided to do different things. I don't want to suggest that one could be radically other than oneself, but one can think that one might have decided, instead of coming to this lecture this evening, to go to a film – 'The Anatomy of Love' I think I saw advertised on the way in from the airport. And in this sense one stands back and sees not only that circumstances might have been different but oneself might be different, and one looks at oneself with an air of relative detachment. And this flows from the fact, and supports the fact, that the reasons which I adopt are never coercive reasons. I always could have decided to act different-ly, and that therefore, even when I have given all the reasons that I can, I can always ask a further question 'All the same, shall I do it?'

This logical gap of autonomy creates the infinite regress of consciousness, the perpetual ability to reflect on one's self. It creates also what one might call the syndrome of the detachment of the ego, which is very common in our own age, particularly I think in people in their early twenties; people being able to see all sorts of arguments for this course and for that course, and see that these are very good arguments, and yet find that they absolutely fail to grip them. They just see themselves as somehow separate and slipping through all the arguments; all the arguments may form a very strong coherent web, but the soul somehow gets through the meshes, and one is left floating and adrift. It is a matter which causes great

114

anguish, great *angst*, to many people, and it arises from the fact that one is conscious of oneself being able to make up one's mind differently, being something different from one's circumstances and from all the arguments which one is bringing to bear on the problem of what one should do. I don't think that this can be argued away, or can be made out to be a bad thing, or anything else; but I would give as a last thought the following one, which I find consoling, and perhaps some of you may. The same reflexiveness of consciousness which makes it possible to suffer from the detachment of the ego also provides the thought reference which gives leverage for the application of Gödel's Theorem, which I think is going to underlie almost any convincing argument for the freedom of the will. That is to say, that what gives us the greatest pain as moral agents also reinstates one of the most basic intimations of consciousness that we are free, and that it is up to us to make up our own minds what we are to do.

Discussion
WADDINGTON
I want to start by entirely agreeing with John Lucas that mind is not the same thing as language and that you can have minds which do not use language. The things nearest to minds, that I'm professionally concerned with as a biologist, are activities in non-human animals, who definitely do not use language. I should certainly dignify many of them by the word 'mind'. Even if you wanted to restrict 'mind' to human mental events, I think anyone who's seen a number of babies before they start talking has no doubt that they are all exceedingly different in their behaviours and their mental operations, and in fact have different minds before acquiring linguistic ability. So I should personally be very willing to go along with John Lucas in saying that language is not by any means the whole of mind. In my talk tomorrow I shall be talking a lot more about mental activities not involving language. But I noticed that John Lucas didn't stay with this point for very long, because when he started to become more positive he immediately started talking about talking again. And I would like to take up his two Latin tags. My Latin is exceedingly rusty. I spent the years from about eight to about fifteen or sixteen learning it, but then I went to another University which is not quite so deeply wedded to lost causes as John Lucas', and I spent the rest of my life forgetting it. So perhaps I could be excused for asking something about, I think it might be, the Chomskyan deep structure of these phrases. '*Loquor ergo es*': I speak, therefore you are. Does this simply mean 'you can hear that I'm talking, therefore there must be somebody around for me to be talking to', or can '*ergo*' be taken in a stronger way, so that the sentence really means 'it's only by my talking to you that you are'? That I think would enshrine a

real fact about mind which we haven't laid sufficient stress on; namely that the human mind as we come across it, and as it talks to us, is a social construction. There is that other classical tag we learnt at school, and I've still got it more or less in mind, even with the wrong pronunciation 'γνῶθι σεαυτόν' know yourself; it may be actually impossible to do so, in the sense that you can't know yourself without knowing a lot about other people as well. It may well be, I think it probably is, the case that the self is not an isolatable thing, that you cannot be an individual isolated, and have a human mind. And in that sense 'loquor ergo es' would carry this much stronger connotation, that you are only brought into being by men talking.

Now the other phrase 'ego ergo ago'. Does this mean only 'here I am, and I can't sit still'? Or does it mean, again using ergo in a strong way (which may be stronger than Latin allows, I don't know) 'I only exist by what I do'? I suggest that that meaning, if it is allowable of the Latin, is an important meaning. And it is very closely allied to what John Lucas was saying in the rest of his talk, because it implies that what I do has a definite enough, a firm enough, character to characterise something's existence, to make something come into existence. Simply messing around, playing around with random activities, could not be said to bring anybody into existence. If you are going to say that actions give rise to the personal existence of a continuing entity which can be called an 'I', then you've got to say these actions are very definite; and I think that means that they have to be actions in search of a certain goal. They have to be directed activities. Now John Lucas lays great stress that we should ourselves select our goals, that we should make up our minds. He seemed to imply that it is only if we ourselves personally make up our minds that our actions can have a definite enough character to be anything more than a random set of movements. I think the biologist would not accept this. Sub-human animals have goals, which they don't make up for themselves in any conscious way. Their goals are basically made up for them by natural selection. It is not, I think, completely necessary for mental activity, for mind, that the goals should be self-selected. I'm going to leave to my two colleagues who deal much more with the human species than I – I'm only a dilettante at the talking animal, I tend to study the non-talking animals – let them take up this point as to whether goal-directed activities, or activities which have a consistent enough character to establish a personal entity, a personal existence, necessarily demand this freewill self-selection of goals that John has been laying so much stress on? I shall be talking again about goal-directed activities tomorrow, in the biological world, and shall have very much less to say about conscious selection.

I want now to come back to a point about language and the bearing it may have on our study of mind, and make a point which I think hasn't yet been sufficiently *clearly* stated. A study of the way we use language is not, as I have said before, anything like a complete account of the way minds work, but I think it may be a very accessible example of one of the ways in which our minds works, open for us to analyse. When we say a sentence, we do it 'spontaneously' – there is some sort of extraordinary telescoping of the process. We don't actually, consciously at least, start off with the deep structure in the Chomskyan sense, work it all out, and decide exactly which words have got to go where, and how to put it all together. We just say the sentence. Now, we don't always say it terribly cleverly or well – we may say it in a highly ambiguous way, and our interolocutors, as Longuet-Higgins said earlier, are usually clever enough to find out roughly what we mean. But we do it in some way in which there's very little gap between the intention and the carrying out of that intention. And I think this is so for a great many consciously directed activities other than language. Lots of things we do we don't actually think out. Take playing a shot at tennis or bicycling, or anything like that; you can't really think out exactly what you are going to do as the ball approaches you across the net. You just do it. And I think this is a rather surprising and peculiar characteristic of what our mental activities can do, the way our minds work. It does have this ability to jump over what looks like an absolute forest of detail. The people who are trying to programme computers to use language, in the sense of making and understanding sentences, are really finding just what exactly is involved in this jumping over the detail, and how you could imagine the mind does it in other contexts, such as controlling muscular activities like hitting tennis balls, and so on. That is going to be, to my mind, one of the important contributions which one is hoping to see come out of the analysis of language. I'm suggesting that there is something very much in common in mechanism between the 'loquor' and the 'ago' in John's phrases. And it seems to me very mysterious what this is, and I am hoping that the computer people will help to tell us something about it.

LUCAS

I'll just make one confession about these two Latin tags, the two lower ones. The first one is quite respectable, it was made up by Descartes, who had been brought up by the Jesuits, and knew Latin properly; the other two were made up by me, who spent the years from eight to eighteen learning Chemistry, and whose Latin is very bad. Therefore don't start quoting them! But what I am going to do is to agree with part of what Waddington said on '*loquor ergo es*'. Of course, it is true, as every mother knows, that babies get turned into people by being talked to. But I also want to argue a second point, that

117

it's not of course simply by my opening my mouth that I can bring you into existence, but rather that if I am talking to you I can thereby show that I am presupposing your existence. It originally came to me arguing with an undergraduate who was trying to get me to prove that he existed. And the mere fact that one talks to a person shows something. The second one, *'ego ergo ago'*, I think shall pass, because I can see two other people who are anxious to be active, and I'll let them be so.

LONGUET-HIGGINS

I want to get behind John Lucas's statements, to what is biting him. It strikes me that what John Lucas is doing is putting a little fence around the autonomy of people, as something we mustn't allow the sciences to study. Somehow or other, we must keep formal description away from this, because it is a sanctuary which somehow is not to be trespassed upon. Now, I'm not one for trampling heavily all over other people's dreams. But I don't think that it works in practice to put hedges round little bits of reality and then say they are not to be investigated. Perhaps I might amplify this point a little bit. John was saying that, when we act, we can consider reasons for taking this action or reasons against taking that one, and we can then make our minds up, but that we aren't in any way constrained by a consideration of the reasons for doing something, and we can't weigh them in a balance and let the outcome determine our action. Well, I'm not quite sure what is being asserted here. One thing which is obvious, of course – and which I was anxious to allow in my thesis of last week – was that when one says something to somebody one says it in a very considerable degree of ignorance about their state of mind, their wishes, their inclinations, their previous experience, and so on. We are extraordinarily ignorant of one another's mental states, and the marvel is that against such odds, we can communicate at all in language. But one of the essential characteristics of human beings, which we share with other animals, is our acute sensitivity to happenings in our environment. If John asks me if I would very kindly shut the door, and at the particular moment a speck of dust gets into my eye, I might very well say 'Wait a moment, I'm awfully sorry, a speck of dust has got into my eye'. Now a speck of dust is a very small thing, and its arrival on the surface of my eyeball is an extraordinarily unpredictable kind of event, and of course this is only one extremely trivial example of the fact that we are, in taking any action, likely to be influenced by so many different things in such a sensitive way that it is hardly surprising that our decisions are not predictable with reference merely to the reasons why one might take a particular course of action or the reasons why one might not.

KENNY

I'd like to say something first of all about the relationship between consciousness and mind. John Lucas began by putting

118

forward, rather nervously, as a difficult thesis which he thought Longuet-Higgins and I would disagree with and pounce on, the thesis that there should be, that there could be, consciousness without language. I don't know what gave him the idea that either Longuet-Higgins or I would have any objection whatever to this thesis. It seems to me a very obvious truth that there can be consciousness without language. Cats and dogs don't speak; cats and dogs see and hear and feel. Seeing, hearing, and feeling are modes of consciousness: therefore there can be consciousness without language.

Anybody who denies this is in some way or other a great fool to deny it. I say, *in some way or other* is a great fool, because of course very clever men have denied it. By a quaint coincidence, perhaps the cleverest man who ever denied it was Descartes, whom John Lucas said he had come here tonight not to bury but to praise, and reinstate. I think that Descartes was clearly wrong in thinking that animals lacked consciousness.

However, I do want to query the equation of mind and consciousness, which was explicitly made, I think, by Waddington, and passively consented to by Lucas. I think that the best way to approach mind is not through consciousness — not, that is to say, if we are interested in the mind as the characteristic of human beings. For consciousness is something which human beings share with non-human beings, whereas there are features which, we have been arguing, they do not share with other creatures. Among ones which have been mentioned, by myself, or by others, at earlier stages, have been the autonomy of human beings (which John Lucas stressed this evening), their ability to reflect upon themselves, their ability to think of distant times and places, their ability to prove Gödel's Theorem, their ability to speak Latin and other such elegant accomplishments. It seems clear to me that all of these abilities, with the possible exception of the ability for autonomous action, presupposes the use of language. As Waddington pointed out, it was very interesting that all John Lucas' examples of the special characteristics of mind were very heavily linguistic. I don't see how a non-language-user, for instance, could have an asymmetry between the first person and the third person pronoun. I don't see how a non-language-user could imagine things long ago, as in Ancient Rome, or have intentions for the non-immediate future, say an intention to catch a train three weeks hence. I don't see how an animal can be self-conscious or reflect upon itself, except by the use of language with its particular reflexive properties.

I don't want to say that we oughtn't to talk about consciousness, because we are supposed to be talking about mind. Clearly this would just be being terminologically obstructive. But I do think that the crucial elements in man's uniqueness as a rational agent are concerned much more

directly with his language-using ability than with the consciousness which he shares with other animals. I've already
argued for one half of this, that there can be consciousness
without mind as in animals. Last week we were talking about
the suggestion made by Chomsky and Freud that there can be
mind without consciousness, that is to say, that many of the
skills and activities which exhibit mentality may not be
conscious, may not be obvious to introspection.

Lucas tended to play down language because he mis-
conceives the relationship between language and thought. He
said that we are really only interested in what people say
because we want to know what they are thinking, unless we
happen to have special professional interests in style or
computer programming. He says language arises because of our
concern with what others are thinking. Now this seems to me a
grotesque travesty of the truth. The great majority of the most
interesting thoughts are thoughts which just couldn't be
thought if there were not language. And all the thoughts to
which Lucas drew our attention were thoughts which could
not be thought without language. If one is going to have
interesting thoughts about mathematics, about religion, about
poetry, about philosophy, about science, one must have a
language to have those thoughts in. It's a great mistake to think
of language as merely the means of communicating to others
thoughts which we could have had for ourselves without
language. Language is just as much a medium for ourselves to
think our own thoughts in as it is a medium for the
communication of thoughts to others.

LUCAS

I will pick up only some of the points. I'm going not to pick
up the speck in Longuet-Higgins' eye, because the beam in my
own will take too long to remove. But I would like to take up
his first point, which I think is of very considerable importance, where he said that I was building a fence around a
sanctuary, and saying 'no' to scientific investigation. And this
turns very much on what we mean by scientific investigation.
It's a point which we raised in our first lecture and then we
had it out over the algorithms. I do think that in one sense of
the phrase 'scientific investigation' there are things about
persons which the scientist cannot, according to that canon,
discover. That is, there is a certain methodology of scientific
investigation which says that all scientific investigations shall
be able to be checked up by anyone. The philosophy of
science is very very democratic, although, as you know, its
sociology in practice is very aristocratic. Anyone can check up
on a scientific statement. And this is not true when we are
dealing with persons, their reasons, their states of mind. This is
the reason why the doctor had the nightmare — there was
something which if the patient was conscious he knew, namely
that it was hurting like anything, and this is a something which

120

is not discoverable by scientific investigation, although it is subsequently made known by the use of the first person singular. Now it depends how far you weigh scientific and how far you weigh personal. I don't want to say that there is something that cannot be known. I do want to say that if it is to be known it's got to be known by the persons concerned revealing it. And there is in this sense something first personal which runs against the *im*personal ideal of scientific investigation, but doesn't run against a more generous view of what the whole of knowledge is like.

I now want to turn to Kenny's remarks, where of course he can pull the mat from under my feet. Everything I've been doing this evening is linguistic − I've been talking − and it's very hard to find a convincing counter-example to the claim that there is no consciousness without the use of language. I had to think a long time to get this example of the patient. It's very difficult to get really clear examples to show what besides language is important, but I think it's very important to do this, and I've just tried to do so on one or two other points. First of all, he was raising the question about it being only by means of language that we can have memories of things long ago. John Locke, in his *Essay on the Human Understanding*, argues that why brutes have minds is that they can remember things, and he instances a particular case: a bird remembering how to sing. Now the example won't work completely − Longuet-Higgins has designed a holophone which will in a sense give some memory reactions, but although Locke's facts I think could be queered, his logic I think is right. That here we can find sometimes with animals, the relative detachment from the stimulus of the existing situation which entitles us to say that this is a phenomenon of consciousness and it's clearly not linguistic. To pick up another point, that whenever we think, we must think by means of language. Well, I beg to doubt this. It depends of course on the first-hand testimony of other people. One of the problems which has beset people who have to read philosophy is that the English Empiricists obviously had very vivid visual imaginations, and weren't particularly good at words. This is why their whole theory of mind is based in terms of images. Other people are very good at words, and have to learn to construct images. But it seems to me clear that some people do think much more in terms of images; mathematicians often think wordlessly, so they tell me. And only later write down squiggles. I myself often think quite hard, and then have a great job trying to find words to express the thought. The Greek formula, 'λόγον 'έχειν τε καὶ διδόναι' gives two things: to have the reason, and to be able to give it in words. And I think it is, although difficult, possible to take cases here where people have reason but haven't yet managed to crystallise it out. And I can only appeal to your experience, either as mathematicians, or as image makers, or as

121

rather inarticulate philosophers, to ask you to join my side.

Finally, since I'm expected to do something polemical on Kenny; where on earth did I get the idea that he and Longuet-Higgins weren't fully paid up subscribing members of the Cartesian doctrine of consciousness? In his rooms in Balliol, when we trying to devise this programme, they had said what they thought, and I had protested against it, and this — 'Consciousness without Language' — was how Kenny expressed my thought.

Ninth Lecture. The Importance of Goals

One of the records we have set up in this marathon series of lectures is to have reached number nine without ever actually saying what we are talking about. That is, nobody has yet attempted to define 'mind'. And I'm not going to try to break that worthy record. The word can be used in a number of different senses; either in a quite restricted sense, referring only to the allegedly rational mind of man, or in a broader sense, referring to mental activities of other animals, and so on. I'm saying this just to warn you that I'm going to use it in rather a broad sense, to cover mental activities, or mind-*like* activities in other animals as well as man.

I agree with John Lucas that it would be frustrating to restrict the use of the word only in reference to conscious language, although one could, of course, write one's dictionary in that form if one wished to. However, the conscious and language-using mind has certainly evolved from non-linguistic mental activities in less highly evolved forms of life. To restrict consideration of mind to its most highly evolved forms is to commit the opposite mistake to reductionism, against which Christopher Longuet-Higgins warned us in his first lecture. We may not always be able to explain the complex by reference only to the simpler — as he reminded us — but I think it is even more true that we cannot hope to understand the complex if we leave the simpler altogether out of account. I shall, therefore, in this lecture start my consideration of the mind by making some remarks about mental activities in less highly evolved organisms than man.

To the biologist the most fundamental question to ask about any aspect — whether it is an activity or an organ — of an organism, is often put in the form 'what is its function?'. This is a shorthand way of asking, in the first place 'how is this particular activity or organ involved in the whole network of activities which enable the organism to keep alive?' And since we know that all living organisms are involved in evolution, that question in itself implies 'what role does this activity or organ play in enabling the organism to reproduce and contribute to the evolutionary history of the population of which it forms a part?' The basic point of Darwin's theory of natural selection, on which the whole of biology is based, is the simple argument that any activity which does not contribute, or contributes ineffectively, to the production of offspring in later generations will in the course of time eventually disappear for that very reason. All activities and

123

organs of biological organisms can therefore be said to serve well or ill the 'goal' of evolutionary transmission. They are all subjected to natural selection, which over the generations tailors them so that they serve this goal better and better.

The goal of leaving offspring throughout periods of evolutionary time can, of course, only be achieved by interactions between organisms and their environment, since an organism must continually obtain new supplies of nutrients, energy and so on, and often must escape from enemies. To pass the test of natural selection an organism must, therefore, always adapt; that is, interact with the environment in which it finds itself in some way which enables it to persist and eventually to reproduce. One can say that any process of adaptation — whether it is a chameleon changing its colour to blend with its surroundings, or a man living in the high Andes growing a larger pair of lungs and a higher concentration of red blood corpuscles in response to the lower oxygen pressure, is brought about by a goal-seeking mechanism, a mechanism which seeks the goal of evolutionary perpetuation.

From this point of view, the more highly evolved types of nervous activity, which control complex behavioural responses to stimuli which impinge on the sense organs from the external world, are subtle and more or less powerful mechanisms for adapting to a variable environment. Evolution has gradually brought into being increasingly complex and effective adaptive mechanisms of this kind. Wherever along this evolutionary sequence we wish to start using the word *mind*, it will still be true that what we are talking about is fundamentally a mechanism for achieving the goal of self-perpetuation or the leaving of offspring over long periods of time. The acquisition of language, at some point in the evolutionary history of man, introduced a new mechanism for adaptation — I think we would all agree, a more powerful mechanism than any other animal has at its disposal to deal with the environment in all its complexity. (I am not proposing to deal with the question whether this is 'progress'. There is, of course, the alternative, for instance, burying oneself in the mud of the sea bed and going on reproducing there without bothering about anything further, a policy which has been satisfactorily followed by certain sea-shells which have remained unchanged since the Cambrian period at the very beginning of the history of cellular life on earth).

The first step in the biological approach to an understanding of mind is, therefore, to enquire what we know in general about adaptive mechanisms and their evolution. I should warn you that what I have to say about this is rather unorthodox. I believe that the processes of evolution, particularly when we talk about more highly evolved organisms, are considerably more complicated, subtle and interesting than they are often supposed to be. During the last 40 or 50 years most biologists

124

seem to have been persuaded to accept almost as unquestionable dogma that evolution can be fully accounted for in terms of two very simple factors: the occurrence of new hereditary variations by a process of gene mutation which takes place entirely at random without rhyme or reason; and the process of natural selection, which amounts to no more than the different efficiencies of organisms in leaving offspring which grow up to contribute to the reproductive population of the next generation.

I believe both statements are true enough as far as they go, but I think neither of them goes far enough to be at all illuminating. They were first propounded and enshrined as dogma at a time when students of heredity had just realised the importance of studying the offspring from crosses between known and carefully selected individual parents, and had, also quite recently, discovered that hereditary characteristics are transmitted by separate discrete identifiable factors, or genes. It is natural that their first step was to try to account for evolutionary processes in terms of that kind; but since then, we have come to realise that in many ways these terms are too simple.

The first over-simplification is to try to talk of evolution in terms of individuals. An individual does not evolve, he dies. Evolution is a phenomenon that takes place at the level of populations, and any theory of evolution must be a theory of populations, not of individuals. This has the consequence of shifting the emphasis away from the particular genes contained in the single individual to questions concerning the whole collection of genes carried by the set of individuals making up the population, i.e. to what is called the 'gene pool of the population'. Now it is certainly true that new genes can only be added to the gene pool by the rare process of random mutation, but gene pools, when studied, turn out to have a more sophisticated character than being just a collection of individual genes. The genes which persist in such a pool, through many generations, are found to be in some way fitted to one another, so that any bunch of them which comes together to form a new individual is likely to give a harmonious individual — the genes are said to be co-adapted. Such co-adapted genes found in a natural population tend to be fitted together to control development in a chreodic way, so that our hands nearly always develop five fingers, even though every one of us contains many different genes and every one of us has developed in rather differing circumstances.

I think that this means that in considering the later stages of evolution, which produce things like complex forms of behaviour and neural activities which we might be tempted to associate with mind, we can almost afford to forget the way in which new individual genes originate. The random nature of gene mutation remains important in very simple organisms like bacteria, and perhaps in the evolution of chemical constituents of the body which are closely related to particular genes, such as identifiable proteins. But when we are considering complex organs like hands or eyes or, still more, brains, the random origin of individual gene mutations seem to me no more important than the random processes which have given rise to the individual stones which make the aggregate formed into concrete blocks. In discussing the architectural differences between a building by say, Le Corbusier and one by Denis Lasdun, one is only peripherally interested in the different aggregates they have specified for their concrete. I do not think it adds much more light to a discussion of the evolution of the human or chimpanzee mind to keep harping back to the random nature of gene mutation.

A second important point in which the neo-Darwinist formulation of evolutionary processes was drastically over-simplified concerns hereditary characters. I have just been talking (as they do) in terms of genes and natural selection, but of course natural selection has nothing directly to do with genes. It is not a set of genes which leaves offspring in the next generation, but an organism developed under the control of those genes. This distinction is known in genetics as that between the *genotype*, which is the collection of hereditary potentialities, and the *phenotype*, which is the entity in which those potentialities come to realisation. Natural selection acts on phenotypes, and phenotypes, of course, have characters which are influenced not only by the hereditary potentialities with which they start but by the environmental circumstances in which those potentialities develop.

A few decades ago, people used to try to make a distinction between 'hereditary characters' which were completely determined by the genetic constitution of the organism, and 'acquired characters' which were completely dependent on the external and environmental circumstances during the development of the organism. In the first flush of excitement at discovering the existence of individual genes, writers about evolution – the so-called neo-Darwinists – argued that only hereditary characters could contribute to the next generation and thus to evolution, and that acquired characters were completely without influence on evolution. It has taken biologists a long time to realise that this must be nonsense, simply because it is impossible to make a distinction between hereditary and acquired characters. Every character of an organism must be 'hereditary' in that it could not have been produced had the organism not had a hereditary potentiality for developing it; similarly every character must be to some extent acquired, in that all development must go on in some environmental circumstances and the final outcome will be influenced in smaller or greater degree by these circumstances. Of course the development of some characters is more easily and obviously influenced by external circumstances than that of others, but that is only a quantitative difference, not a difference in principle.

If the development of an organism is affected by its environment in a manner which improves the chance that the organism will succeed in leaving offspring, this will obviously increase its contribution to later evolution, that is to say its natural selective value. In fact we can say that natural selection will favour organisms which acquire useful characteristics. Now, if one combines this simple fact with the rather more unexpected one I mentioned in my first lecture, namely that developmental processes are difficult to alter, one finishes up with a very powerful evolutionary mechanism. Say we have a population of animals which has to meet some new challenge offered to it by an altered environment, there may be some individuals in the population whose development is changed by the environment in a way which makes them better able to deal with the challenge — they show a capacity for adaptive modification. They will, therefore, be favoured by natural selection. After this selection has gone on for some consider- able number of generations the new pathways of development will have gradually acquired a more pronounced chreodic character which can itself be difficult to modify. In fact should the environment now revert to what it was before the whole process started, the organism may well go on developing in the way in which it adapted to the changing environment. This process, which I have called genetic assimilation, gives exactly the same end result as the theory proposed by Lamarck, at one time espoused by Darwin but rejected by modern biology, of the direct inheritance of required charac- ters.

The fact that by a slightly more sophisticated development of modern biology we have come across an evolutionary mechanism which can produce the same effect, is I think not without importance in relation to mind. It shows how a behavioural pattern, which in an earlier evolutionary stage emerged only in the actual presence of a certain environmental situation, might if it was selected as useful over many generations, become habituated to a chreodic developmental pathway which would operate even in the absence of that environmental situation. It is because of the existence of this mechanism that I am not alarmed by the suggestions of people like Chomsky, that man has an 'innate' capacity for the use of language. If at an early stage in his evolution it was useful for an individual to be able to adapt to a language-using community, i.e. to learn language as fast as possible, selection for this capacity might well have brought about a genetic assimilation of at least the bases for what had originally been only a learned adaptive response.

The third great oversimplification of the neo-Darwinist statement of evolution implies that the thing that is being selected (genotype according to the conventional statement, phenotype as I suggest) finds itself inevitably subjected to certain selective pressures, arising from 'its environment'. In fact most higher organisms select their environment before they allow the environment to select them. Release a hare and a rabbit in the middle of a field, the rabbit will run off to the hedge and live its life there, while the hare will be content to live its life in the open field. Even plants, in a more rudimentary way, make some sort of selection of the circumstances in which they will develop. If a seed falls on stony ground in the desert, it simply refuses to germinate until the next shower of rain comes along and gives it an environment at least somewhat appropriate to its needs. However, there can be no doubt that this reciprocal relationship of mutual feedback, between an organism which selects an environment and an environment which then selects the most efficient organisms, assumes greater importance as we go higher up the evolutionary scale.

In particular, I think it must be of crucial importance in the evolution of behavioural patterns and of anything which we might call a mind. For instance, at some point in their evolutionary history, the ancestors of horses began to eat primarily the grasses of open plains, and not for instance the leaves of shrubs. They then had to deal with the possibility of being attacked by carnivores, and they came to deal with this threat by running away rather than by standing on their hind legs and trying to fight off the attack with their front feet, as giraffes do, for instance. One might somewhat figuratively say that they had 'chosen' to inhabit one type of environment rather than the other, and to adopt one type of strategy against predators rather than another. But, of course, that mode of expression should not be taken to imply a conscious process of choice. However, once evolution had started to go in those directions, this defined the character of the natural selection that would be exerted, and evolutionary changes went on in the same direction for a very long period. The mind of the horse has evolved into that of a plains-dwelling fleet-footed animal, which runs away from its enemies. The mind of the buffalo, on the other hand, is that of a plains-dweller which faces its enemies and charges them.

Such types of animal minds, evolved in relation to a reciprocal interaction between the selection of environment by animal and of animal by environment, are what we refer to rather crudely as instincts. An instinct is a pattern of behaviour which is to a major extent dependent on the hereditary constitution of the animal. It is a mistake, however, to think that it is in all cases wholly dependent on the genetic constitution, and that the environment plays no role in shaping the behaviour. I do not want to discuss the science of animal behaviour, so I will mention only one example which illustrates two ways in which the environment is important in the development of instinct. In my first lecture I mentioned weaver birds, who build elaborate nests consisting of a completely enclosed nest chamber, approached through a tubular entrance. Each species of weaver birds builds nests of a different shape. I do not know why different species should adopt differently shaped homes, but the fact that they do shows that there is a very strong hereditary element in their behaviour. However, birds build a better finished, and more competently constructed, nest in their second year than they do in their first. There is, therefore, an element of learning involved. Consider the problem of a bird approaching a half finished nest. It has got to decide just how to weave the piece of straw in its beak in amongst the other pieces of straw. It has been found there are certain kinds of weaving stitches which it can do, but it never, for instance, ties a proper knot. However, it has always to discover some way of adapting the particular types of weaving process at its command to the particular circumstances which confront it. This involves highly adaptive behaviour; much more adaptive to the environment than one might imagine if one simply wrote the instincts down as hereditary.

We may say that instinctive behaviour is behaviour related to a rather well-defined goal, but often demanding a more flexible adaptive type of behaviour, including the possibility of learning from experience, in deciding exactly how that goal shall be reached. I myself should not refuse to use the word *mind* in connection with organisms which showed this type of behaviour. The main point I should like to emphasise is that in such cases the goal towards which the instinct drives has certainly not been decided by any conscious choice of the organism, but by this subtle evolutionary process of natural selection within a framework which has been set by the previously existing instinctive behaviour.

I think it might be argued that certain computer programmes have already reached, or are about to reach, this level of instinctive mind-like behaviour, reaching a goal which has been set for them by some outside agency. For instance, Winograd's programme for understanding English sentences is comparable at best to an instinctive mind in that its goal was not set for it by itself, but by somebody else, namely its programmer. But in achieving this goal it shows some of the flexibility and capability of learning of the kind we have seen in the weaver bird.

In man, evolution has produced a mind at a different and higher level of complexity, namely a rational mind. Piaget, that great student of the development of the human mind during childhood, argues that the rational mind involves two faculties which have rather different relations to the external world, and that it is only by the combination of these two faculties that it reaches such a degree of efficiency that it makes up almost the whole of man's mind and reduces his instinctive activities to a very minor component. The two faculties Piaget distinguishes are, firstly, the ability to learn from experience, and secondly, an appreciation of logical mathematical theorems. To learn from experience is surely to adopt new ways of behaving — to write new programmes, if you like — which are adapted to achieving some goal in the light of the surrounding circumstances. One can easily see that it could become, and in man it has become, an extremely flexible and powerful way of achieving goals. But do we need to invoke another separate faculty of appreciating logico-mathematical relations? Could we not regard them also as the results of learning from experience? Piaget argues that this is not good enough. Although in practice a child may have to learn by experience that you cannot have a triangle in which one side is longer than the sum of the other two sides, yet this logico-mathematical relationship would remain true whether the child learnt it or not. The learning, he says, is in this case merely becoming acquainted with a relationship which is not dependent on what happens to go on in the environment. When the child learns that larger things tend to be heavier than smaller ones, he is really reaping the fruits of experience; but when he learns that $2 + 2 = 4$ he is merely becoming acquainted with something which is essentially independent of experience. I am not sure whether to accept this argument of Piaget's or not. If one does, there is a great difficulty, which I do not think Piaget can quite resolve, in trying to decide how these logico-mathematical relationships enter into our mind.

These two faculties of Piaget's are of course supported by, indeed probably dependant on, the ability to use language. But I also would like to leave on one side, because I feel quite incompetent to deal with it, the very interesting problem of the relations between learning from experience and logico-mathematical relationships on the one hand and semantics and grammar in linguistics on the other. I suspect there are close parallels between these two pairs, and perhaps some of the linguists here will be able to enlighten us about them.

I should like to conclude by going back to the problem of goals. As we have seen, the goals of instinctive mentalities are determined by the evolutionary natural selective processes which I have sketched. The goals of rational minds appear to be set by those minds themselves. John Lucas seemed indeed to wish to make this the fundamental definition of a rational mind. There is, of course, another current of thought, the deistic, which would maintain that the long-term goals for man are set by the will of God, and that the goals or purposes which a rational mind may set before itself at any given time, are to be regarded as partial short term goals, which may well be mistaken. I think we can discuss the formation of goals in man's rational mind only if we recognise that there are goals of longer and shorter term, and of greater and lesser degree of compellingness. Introspection certainly seems to show us that we can perceive a certain situation and formulate a conscious goal with respect to it, and we shall then judge behaviour as rational or not, according to whether it tends to the achievement of that goal. I do not at this point want to raise the question whether the formulation of such conscious goals demands free will or not. I want instead to emphasise the fact that the goals are formulated in relation to certain sets of circumstances. I agree with John Lucas that the ability to formulate such goals − to make up one's mind as he says − is an essential, and probably the most essential, aspect of the functioning of minds at the rational level.

I want now to raise the question, could we imagine a machine, a computer, which achieves this degree of rationality? I do not think anyone has yet done so, and I am not certain whether anyone is even trying to do so. However, I see no reason in principle why it should not be done, at least within some specific context. This context would correspond to the adoption of a specific strategy of survival, such as the horse's strategy of running away. In such a context, it seems to me that the goal implied by the context might be deduced simply from examining the causal relations between the components. I will use an analogy which first occurred to me many years ago. If a Martian were dropped out of his flying saucer and landed in a deserted bassoon factory, and was able to look around at the various bits and pieces, and experiment to see how they fitted together, it seems to me that he would be able to come to the conclusion that the goal of the whole set-up was to manufacture bassoons, even if he had never heard or thought of such an instrument before. Or, consider the *Project MAC* set-up used by Winograd. There is a set of rectangular blocks of different colours, and apparatus for receiving information about an image of them reduced to dimensions, and an arm for manipulating them, provided with rectangular movements in three dimensions of space. Surely a computer would be able to come to the conclusion that the goal of the whole set up is to move the blocks about, along linear paths in space, possibly piling them one on top of the other, but not for instance rotating them or trying to turn them inside out.

So there is a possibility, I think, that even a computer could formulate a goal. Could it formulate a sensible goal? Well, let's have another example. Suppose you had a computer, and fed into it the whole international air schedule time-tables, so that it had all the information about all the scheduled air flights from anywhere to anywhere. Then you put into it simply the input, let's say Edinburgh-Athens, and say 'go ahead'. It might inspect what it has got in its memory, and what could be done, and it might possibly come up with the answer that the quickest way of going from Edinburgh to Athens is as follows ... But it might also come up with the longest way to go from Edinburgh to Athens, without going to any one place more than once. You could cover the globe up and down, and have a wonderful time going from Edinburgh to Athens. And there would be nothing in particular, in the set-up so far, by which it could decide which of those two goals made sense. But if you then went up to another level of complexity, and also said that the output from that stage has got to be fed into another operation, in which only three months' time is allowed, there is another engagement somewhere else, only a certain amount of money, and so on, the computer might well – it would, I think – be able to come to the conclusion that the goal of the longest possible journey didn't make sense when it had to be referred to the next stage; And the goal that did make sense, referred to the next stage, was the shortest time.

If this is accepted, then computers might be expected to achieve the modest amount of rationality involved in formulating goals related to defined but unexplained sets of circumstances. Should they ever succeed in doing so, this would certainly be a long step towards the achievement of mind in machines. However, two further steps would remain before machines achieved anything really comparable to the mind of man.

The first is one which perhaps man himself has not yet fully succeeded in taking; that is, to define a goal in relation, not to a small selection of the circumstances in the surrounding universe, but rather to the universe as a whole. If one believes that a goal is inherent in a set of circumstances – or to put it theologically, that God's will is immanent in his creations – then the ultimate task for the rational mind is to discover what that goal is. This, the discovery of natural ethics, or natural religion is, surely, the greatest endeavour which mankind is still engaged in – as indeed Adam Gifford must have thought when he endowed these lectures.

The other aspect of human mind which this discussion has left out of account is the non-rational parts of it. I mean the appreciations of beauty, the emotions of joy, sorrow and so on. It seems to me that all those aspects of mind which are concerned with controlling reactions to experienced circumstances might in principle be carried out by machines capable of computation and perception in the sense of developments of modern computers; but the aesthetic and emotional aspects of the mind seem something quite different and our discussions of rationality and language should not tempt us to forget them entirely.

Discussion

KENNY

Professor Waddington's lecture, which is the last of the full length lectures this year, has provided us with a very good lead in to next year's topic, which, as I think you know, is to be *The Development of Mind.* He has already shown us some of the problems that we are going to meet when we try to connect the notion of mind with that of evolution and development. But he is obviously right that we haven't yet achieved the task that we set ourselves for this year, even this small-term, self-selected goal, of talking about the *nature* of mind. We haven't been able to come up with a satisfactory, agreed, definition of what it is for something to have a mind.

Now I think that the disagreements between us, at least between Waddington and myself, are partially just terminological, but partially concern a matter of substance. I mean that the question whether animals other than human animals have minds is partially a terminological issue. In the terminology which Professor Waddington favours, men have rational minds and other animals – and he thinks perhaps insects – have non-rational minds, whereas in the terminology that I favoured men and perhaps intelligent Martians, if there are any, have minds, and animals have consciousness, but not minds – with the possible exception, of course, of Washoe, who is between the two. If she really has got language, and can really develop the language to something like a human level, then it wouldn't surprise me to learn that she was able to exhibit the defining characteristics of mind. Now, so far, as I say, this is just a matter of terminology, because we both of us attribute consciousness to animals. We both of us, with some slight hesitation, preserve language to man. We both think that language and consciousness are of importance with regard to the definition of mind. Where we differ, of course, is in where we place the emphasis. I think that language is much more essential to mentality than consciousness is, and Professor Waddington takes the opposite point of view.

The substantial point of disagreement, I think, is this: why do we call the things that we want to call minds – why do we want to call them 'mental'? What is the criterion by which something is 'mental'? And, in particular, what is the relation between having a mind and displaying the nervous structure or patterns of behaviour on which we base the judgement that something has a mind? Is the relation between mind and behaviour a necessary one, or a contingent one? Are these signs of mentality, like the use of language, part of what is meant by 'having a mind', or are they just bits of, perhaps very convincing, inductive evidence? Now, I think the former. I

133

think that to have such properties as the ability to use language, to do mathematics, and so on, is just what is meant by 'having a mind', and that these aren't mere inductive evidence suggesting that things have minds. I think that Waddington is inclined to think that the exhibition of adaptive behaviour in animals is inductive evidence for their having mind. If he thinks that, the question arises: 'what is this mind that it is inductive evidence for — what is the hypothesis to which these bits of evidence are relevant?' And I think the hypothesis is, that these animals, perhaps even insects, have a certain essentially private inner something which is rather like the certain essentially private inner something which *I* have, and which only I really know that I have.

This is an important point of disagreement between us, because I think that this is the point at which Waddington takes the step out of biology, into mythology. This notion of the essentially private mind, the something within to which I alone have a privileged access, which is a set of experiences which I cannot communicate to others — this is a myth created principally by Descartes. Or perhaps I am exaggerating the genius of Descartes: it is a myth which is perhaps part of human nature, but a myth which Descartes first gave detailed philosophical shape to. He did so specially in the *Meditations*, to which John Lucas alluded yesterday: the meditations of a lonely spirit, doubting the existence of the world, doubting the existence of his own body, trying so far as possible to be a lonely, isolated point, independent of any other mind (except, as it in the end turned out, the mind of God — but independent of any other created mind) for its knowledge of truth, for the meaningfulness of the language that it used.

Descartes, beside creating this, as I think, mythical entity, showed that the only evidence there could be for the existence of a mind of this kind was the use of language. And because animals don't use language, he therefore concluded that animals don't have this kind of mind. Wittgenstein, who is often thought of as being somebody who refuted Descartes, in a way just continued this part of Descartes' work. He showed that even language didn't provide sufficient evidence for the existence of this sort of private mind. He therefore concluded that human beings didn't have it either — indeed, that it was altogether mythical, because a mind which is to have the type of thoughts which Descartes has in his *Meditations*, must be a mind which possesses a language, and, Wittgenstein argued, a language is something which presupposes at least a potential community of language-users.

I'd just like to go back to a point made last night. It was clear that when I said, following Wittgenstein, that thought presupposed language, I was misunderstood by John Lucas, who took me to mean that every time I think a thought the actual thought must be formulated in words in my consciousness. I didn't mean this at all: I meant that thoughts of any complexity are thoughts which presuppose the *possession* of a language, though of course they need not be formulated in words at the time when I think them. Let me give a terribly simple example of this. As I was walking along the Canongate this morning, I saw a notice above a shop, which said 'Thistle Freezers'. And I was puzzled by this – I thought, why should anyone want to freeze thistles? And then I thought, oh, of course, I'm in Scotland, and the thistle is a heraldic symbol. It's a brand name; it means not *thistle* freezers, but thistle *freezers*. Now the point of this trivial story is that this thought, which has taken me several seconds to relate, went through my mind in a flash like that. I didn't enunciate all these words, *sotto voce*, as I had the thought, yet it is also clearly a thought that nobody who didn't know a language – indeed, nobody who didn't know English – could ever have had. I think that not even John Lucas would think that cats and dogs, for all we know, are going around having thoughts of just that kind, only the poor things can't tell us about them.

Just a final point, about the evolutionary part of Waddington's paper. I have some difficulty about the notion of evolution of language, but I don't want to develop this point because it's something which we shall have to consider in detail next year. I was interested that in his paper, when he was formulating an evolutionary account of language, he said that it might be that natural selection might favour people who adapted well to a language-using community. I've no doubt that it might, but of course this presupposes the existence of a language-using community, and the origin of the language-using community is something that remains to be explained. Though I share in Waddington's belief in the importance of goals for mentality, I find it hard to follow him in the belief that we might be able to detect a goal of the universe as a whole. If there is a Maker of the universe, and he tells us what his goal is, then well and good. But I don't think that we, like Martians dropped into the bassoon factory of the world, can work out a universal goal from our surroundings. I don't think the Martians could, unless they knew what it was to play a bassoon. I think that one cannot work out what is the end-point of a cyclical operation unless one is in a position to make some sort of value-judgement about the different stages of the cycle. I think that if somebody were to just study the evolutionary cycle in the world, they might well come to the conclusion that the world was a factory for producing corpses. Some corpses take longer to produce than others, but after all that is the climax, at the moment after the strivings of the evolutionary process and the strivings of nature during the preparation of the corpse. Once the corpse is produced, the striving ends, and the product is allowed to disintegrate.

135

WADDINGTON

Let me reply very briefly, to give time for Christopher and John. Let me say, first of all, that I do *not* insist on the importance of consciousness for mind. I happen to think that there is a lot of consciousness about in the world – but I haven't any very good grounds for that except logical grounds, and normally I don't find it necessary to ask myself whether a mouse is conscious, or an insect is conscious or not. Again, let me say that I tend to agree with Wittgenstein. I don't think of the mind as an entity. You asked, if I say something has got a mind, what would this be evidence for? It is not evidence for the existence of any sort of entity. I should tend to say things have mind, or engage in mental activity, if their behaviour, if their reacting to stimuli, is much more complex than simple reflexes. So long as I can see that they are reacting to stimuli, and the reaction to the stimulus is not a bit obvious to me, if I can't see how they came to do such an extraordinary thing as building a nest, then I might say this is a mental activity. It is really a name for a type of neural behaviour more complex than one can easily fathom. I don't think you used mind in that very broad sense. You want to confine it to a particular type of complex nervous activity, namely language-use; well, perhaps you would not totally confine it to that, but aren't you really saying that things which don't have language don't have minds, in the way that you and I do.

LONGUET-HIGGINS

I was very much interested indeed in what Waddington said. I agree very much that the idea of a goal is an integral part of the concept of mind; and so is the idea of 'intention'. An organism which can have intentions I think is one which could be said to possess a mind. And intention demands, it seems to me, more than just having a goal, because you might say bacteria had, in some sense, a goal – I mean, to grow, and divide, and so forth. But I think the concept of intention goes beyond this, and involves the idea of the ability to form a plan, and make a decision – to adopt the plan. The idea of forming a plan, in turn, requires the idea of forming an internal model of the world. And in a more sophisticated sort of internal model, of course, there must be room for a model of yourself. And that is where self-consciousness, I think, begins, and gets important. But an internal model of the world, roughly speaking, has to be an abstraction from the world, which, roughly speaking, tells you what the world is likely to do to you if you behave in such and such a way. And, of course, if we live in a community and have to deal with one another, so we want to know how other people are going to behave if we treat them in such and such a way. And language is one of the highest culminations of this progression, from goals, through plans and intentions, to the ability to communicate our plans and intentions and desires and goals to one another. I think that to draw a line somewhere up the evolutionary scale, and say that animals below the line haven't got minds, and that those above have, is rather like trying to draw a sharp line between being asleep and being awake. There are degrees of wakefulness and awareness, and I think it is the same with the mind, language being its highest manifestation, as far as we can tell.

LUCAS

I shall quarrel with Waddington for not quarrelling enough with Kenny, who treated him very unfairly, and put forward the fork of either turning Waddington into a behaviourist, or else into an inductivist, and at one moment was, as Kenny is very fond of doing, discovering behind Wad's outward and visible appearance a Cartesian bogey. Once, when he was younger, Kenny wrote a thesis attacking the Cartesian errors of one Lucasius, who he believed was a tall old gentleman with a white beard. But I think that Waddington gave away too much in saying of course he is only interested in behaviour. He isn't only interested in behaviour. He's interested in behaviour for a reason, that it seems to be mindlike, and there is a certain logical gap here, which I think is rather important for our understanding of mind. First of all, it seems to me quite clear that when we come across purposive behaviour we think that it does suggest that there *is* a reason – that the weaver birds are doing something, because we can assimilate, we feel we can ask the weaver bird 'Why are you doing this?' And it will answer our question with a sentence beginning 'In order to do this, that, and the other'. That is to say, purposes seem to be mind-like because in our own experience a purpose is an acceptable answer to the question of 'why?', 'why are you doing it?', but it is not a sufficient condition of being mind-like, because it is not the only answer. And the reason why there is a certain amount of difficulty, which Kenny was exploiting, is that although it is suggestive of there being a mind that we see a purpose, it isn't conclusive. This is why the homeostatic mechanisms, like thermostats, and so on, which have been discovered by some mathematicians recently, seem to be rather worrying. This is why a hundred years ago the theory of natural selection seemed to be rather worrying. It seemed to be giving an alternative explanation of how a purpose was achieved. And therefore in our understanding of the nature of mind, I think we shall be right to say that to be able to have purposes is a characteristic feature, but it is not a defining feature. We also expect these purposes to be explained, given reasons; I slightly disagree with Longuet-Higgins in his definition of intention. I think intentions are different both from reasons and from purposes. Essentially purposive behaviour is suggestive of there being a mind, but not conclusive if we want to know more fully what sort of reasons there are for having these purposes.

WADDINGTON

I rather like Christopher's introduction of something like intention as well as plan. 'Goals' is certainly too broad a word to use — as he says, you can have goals for bacteria and so on, and nobody would think of giving them minds. Something like intention — as John has pointed out, intention may not be quite the right word, but something of that kind.

Now, as regards the point that John was making. I am of course professionally an embryologist, and nothing is more obviously purposeful than an egg turning itself into a chicken, and yet — this looks purposeful, but it isn't really purpose. If you took it as purpose, this is certainly not enough to allow you to attribute a mind to it. I think that mind has got to have something akin to purpose, of the same general nature as purpose, and I think it has got to be tied up with the nervous system. I'm afraid I'm materialist enough for that. I'm not going to give anything a mind that hasn't got a nervous system. Now I don't say those two points are quite enough to define mind, but at least those two seem to me to be necessary.

Tenth Lecture. Conclusions

Decision

LONGUET-HIGGINS

I have chosen 'decision' as a subject, because I think it is a topic we didn't really do justice to last time, and also because yesterday evening, when we were meeting over sherry, some of you seemed to be interested in this being pursued. So I'd like, if I may, to try and explore a very quick train of thought – it won't take me more than two or three minutes – and then I expect it'll be pounced upon by my colleagues, and they will tear it to shreds. But anyway, here goes.

For me, a decision is a sort of turning-point in a mental process. A mental process, of course, is something very complex. One thing I'd like to stress – and this has been said many times – is that when you think about the mind you are thinking about something *happening*, rather than a static, jelly-like entity. The idea of mind essentially involves ideas of process. Well, let's think of a decision as a turning-point in a process – in a mental process. And the concept of process is almost inseparable from that of mind. You may remember that I was trying to stress the idea of process in suggesting how we might get a better understanding of the mind; and there's a special way of describing processes, which is familiar to mathematicians and such people, and that is by what is called an algorithm. So let's say that a process is what can be specified by an algorithm. A typical algorithm will be a recipe for making a soufflé, or the routine for long division. I'll give you another, non-cooking, non-mathematical algorithm in a moment. If you want to represent an algorithm, you will find it convenient do do so in a programming language. Indeed, programming languages are designed exactly for this purpose. One of them, a well-known one, is called ALGOL – it's rather an ugly name, but what it stands for is 'algorithmic language'. If you have represented an algorithm in this language, you have written a program. And a program is something which you can actually run on a computer – this is where the computer comes in. It is important to realise that a computer program is essentially an abstraction. The computer scientist talks about the computer as a bit of 'hardware', and he talks about programs, by contrast, as 'software.' It's a misleading contrast, of course, because software isn't 'soft' in any sense. It's abstract as opposed to concrete, really; in discussing algorithms we are discussing something extremely abstract, not something concrete. Now, of course, our mental processes take place in our brains – so our minds are to our brains, in a certain sense, what software is to hardware. That's a rather facile comparison, but it'll do.

I said I'd write up an algorithm. This is where the idea of a decision comes in. Supposing you had the job of filling a bucket with stones, then the following algorithm would actually work, as I think you'll see. First of all, 'start' and then proceed by first of all asking a question – 'Is the bucket full?' The answer may be 'Yes', in which case 'Stop'. Or, it may be 'No' – in which case, 'Put in another stone' and proceed back to the question. So the algorithm has a decision point – the point at which the question is answered. The interesting thing about computers, and algorithms written for them – is that you can write for them algorithms which have tests in them. I have said all this because there's obviously been some misunderstanding about where computers come into this story at all. I brought them in because of the most obvious characteristic of what we call the mind is that we have thoughts. And if one wants to describe these at the correct level of abstraction, one has to do so algorithmically – otherwise there is no way of describing them that I can see. And these algorithms can be expressed in a very precise and unambiguous manner as programs which can be run on computers for testing purposes, and that's why the computer analogy is helpful.

WADDINGTON
This seems to me to be a very, very low level of decision. You could call it a decision if you like; but couldn't you programme your computer simply by saying 'Go on putting stones into the bucket until one falls off, then stop'. Then it wouldn't have to decide anything until it came to the end of the process. It seems to me you formulated your recurrent decisions in terms of asking a question – do you stop, or don't you stop? But you could have programmed it in simply – 'Go on doing what you are doing until eventually something happens, and then you stop'. I should use – you might say I should want to use – the word 'decision' for something which you might call 'decision' too, such as 'decide whether you are going to fill the bucket with stones or with water'. I'd want to use 'decision' really as a crest between two chreods. One stable system of behaving here, and another stable system of behaving there, and you decide which of these routines you will go into.

LONGUET-HIGGINS
With the second point I completely agree, but something presumably will decide you to go into one or the other. And that'll be the circumstances prevailing at the time. As to the first point – in fact if you want to implement the concept of going on *until* the bucket overflows, you must keep your eyes open all the time, so that you don't fail to notice when the

bucket overflows. So you've got to be constantly looking, and that is exactly what this programme is in fact doing. It looks every time you put a stone in, to see whether the bucket is full to overflowing. I mean, you could say 'If the bucket overflows, then you've gone on too far' – but that's a trivial point – a trivial difference, really. But an 'until' statement can't be implemented on a computer without a recurrent test to see if the condition is satisfied.

KENNY
I don't think you really have dealt with Waddington's point, have you? This is only a decision in the sense in which I suppose you might say a leaf which is being blown by the wind, first one way and then another, makes the decision to go one way and then the other. If you want to say that, I don't object to your usage. It's bizarre, but that's your own affair. Are you really saying that computers make decisions only in the sense that a leaf makes a decision when it goes one way or the other? If so, I don't think a computer is a very good model for a mind.

LONGUET-HIGGINS
Well, I don't understand in what sense the leaf can be represented by an algorithm with conditional jumps. I mean, if you –

WADDINGTON
It's not a leaf falling – it's a leaf blowing backwards and forwards.

KENNY
Yes. If the wind was blowing that way, it moves that way, and if the wind moves another way, it moves the other way. Well, I mean – do you say 'Have you hit the ground yet – if so, stop'?

LONGUET-HIGGINS
Well, we can of course view the whole operation of a computation running on a computer as a deterministic affair. If you describe it at that level, and talk about the hardware changing its state, then there isn't any question of decisions being made. But the same thing could be said of your brain, at least in my view. On the other hand, that's not the illuminating way to describe the situation. And I think the question is, how is the situation best described, so that we can understand it. And I think that for a leaf falling it isn't an illuminating way of describing it, to say that the leaf is constantly making decisions. It somehow seems to be a description which is not called for by that situation.

LUCAS
Well, it may be illuminating, and it may be illuminating for you – and I think I can see why. It is picking up one aspect, which is quite an important one. Roughly, you are thinking first of all of continuous processes, and their nodes, at which either one thing or another thing can happen. This will work both for what the computer is doing and for what people are doing. Decisions are the critical points when you can go either

to the right or to the left. That part of the analogy, I can see, is illuminating; but I don't think it otherwise is illuminating, because it leaves out a great many points which we feel are important. I find it very difficult to say what a decision is, but one point is, I think, that it is something which one would give a reason for.

LONGUET-HIGGINS

Well, as applied to human beings I couldn't disagree with that – and indeed, yesterday, you remember, when we were talking about decision I wanted to say that I thought the distinctive characteristic of mind – mental activity as opposed to any other sort of activity – was that you had intentions. You intended to do what you did. And this idea is not captured here at all. I agree with you, but I think that the concept of a decision is one which is valuable in this connection, and can be applied in this context without violating the meaning of the word. Whereas I think it would not be possible to maintain that there was any sense in which the bucket-filling program *intended* to make that decision.

KENNY

But you do have an answer – don't you? – to John's point, which I think is a perfectly correct one, that a decision in the only interesting sense is something for which reasons can be given. Because I understand that you have programs – a program that you play noughts and crosses with – which does something rather like giving reasons.

LONGUET-HIGGINS

Yes indeed, that is so. Stephen Isard and I have been writing programs in which we can play a game, noughts and crosses, with the program and then say 'Why did you do that?' And the answer can be 'Because if I had not you could have won'. That sort of thing. And we are trying to put such sentences together in a principled linguistic fashion, by examining the meanings of the words, and the English syntax, and so forth. We are trying to capture the idea of a reason for doing something. The reasons offered by the program are reasons in a rather primitive, crude sense, but they don't refer as yet to a high level goal of which the program itself is aware. The program's higher level goals are in fact set for it by the programmer.

Consciousness

WADDINGTON

It seems to me that consciousness is a subject we haven't discussed sufficiently, and I was accused by Tony of having some rather peculiar views about it. He said that he thought I believed that consciousness an essential criterion of mind; that consciousness is an essential characteristic of a thing if we are to attribute mind to it. Now I find this quite difficult to answer for a reason which will come out in a second — one of the reasons, that is. But let me say first that, if consciousness were to be adopted as a criterion of mind, it would be a signally useless one, because the only way to tell whether any other thing is conscious is to ask it. And that you can only do to human beings; you can't ask a rabbit or a mouse whether it is conscious or not. I therefore think that really the concept of consciousness is not applicable to anything but a language-using animal. Now, you may say in opposition to that — well, you anaesthetize rats and rabbits, and so on, in the lab, and you are quite confident that you make them unconscious. And in a way one is, but actually one is simply overplaying one's hand at this point. One is using an anaesthetic which in man, at least, abolishes consciousness before it abolishes muscular movement. You are not using this drug which John told us about as a sort of horror story of the anaesthetized but conscious person. You are using one of the standard anaes-thetics. And then, really by analogy with what happens in man, you go on until your rat is completely immobilised. Muscular movement has been put out, and you then imagine that its consciousness, if it is conscious, will have been put out. And if, when it recovers after any operation, it shows no sign of having had a traumatic pain experience, evidence supports you. But you are really only hypothesising that it is conscious in the first place; you can't really obtain any factual evidence. You can't ask it, and it can't tell you.

The second point I want to make about consciousness is that it does seem to me the key *private* thing about mind. You can talk to another person about what you are conscious of, but this is communication about consciousness. You can't communicate the consciousness itself. If you did, it would be like communicating things. If I could communicate my consciousness of this paper in front of me, the person I communicated it to would have the *same* experience of the piece of paper that I had. He may be conscious of something, seen from his point of view, and I may be able to describe aspects of my consciousness of it, and talk about it. But I can't communicate *it*.

One question one must ask — again, I think, attributed to me by Tony at one point, is: where does consciousness arise from? Our definitions of the normal material objects we talk about, such as atoms, or anything else of that kind, contain no reference to consciousness. We say consciousness is tied up with activities of our brains, and our brains are made up of atoms, but it seems to me that there is no way of passing from a normal scientific definition of an atom to any conclusion, or any consequence, about consciousness. Scientific definitions of the atom are in terms of its interactions with other material bodies. And to my mind there is a complete conceptual gap between any type of material interaction, however complex,

143

and self-awareness. I don't see that it is any good saying 'oh well, the brain is a very complicated arrangement of atoms, and they therefore can become conscious'. That is begging a question which is really unbeggable. If there is a complete conceptual gap between material entities and consciousness, one conclusion that has been drawn, for instance by White-head, was that, as we know there is consciousness somewhere, namely in ourselves, then something in some way akin to it must be in *all* entities; not that all entities have a consciousness as developed and evolved as our own, but there must be some property of them, from which consciousness could have evolved. That is a logical argument, which I find not very easy to refute. But I suspect that the whole question arises really from some sort of an improper formulation of the subject to begin with. I don't feel in the slightest able to expound this at all clearly — but our primitive experience is a consciousness of *something*; I don't think you can be conscious without being conscious of something. Normally we are conscious of experiences, of occasions of experience, in which there is conscious-ness, and in which there may be sticks and stones and trees, and what have you. Then we break up this experience into the sticks and stones on the one side, and the perceiving conscious subject on the other. I think it's when we break the primitive experience up in this way that we force ourselves to this paradoxical question, where does the consciousness come from — it can't come from the material that we leave on the other side of the equation. But this, I think, is getting beyond the philosophical capacities of the simple biologist, and it's time we heard some more about it from a professional.

LONGUET-HIGGINS
Could I just put in a short remark? One *sufficient* condition for having been conscious at a particular time is that one can remember afterwards what was going on at that time.
WADDINGTON
Is that really true? I thought that people could remember things that they didn't actually perceive at the time.
LONGUET-HIGGINS
Well, perhaps they can, but certainly it's not a matter of common experience. Whereas it is very much a matter of common experience that if you can remember what was happening at noon you can't have been asleep at the time. It seems to me that you've talked about consciousness in two senses. One was consciousness as being awake, as opposed to being asleep; whereas you also spoke about self-consciousness, and I think that raises rather a different set of questions. It's arguable that —
WADDINGTON
No, I wasn't really meaning consciousness in the sense of reflecting, 'well, am I now conscious or not?'

144

LUCAS

Even so, there are I think a number of important distinctions. You took 'consciousness' and 'being conscious of' as though they were quite the same, but I think quite often I'm not conscious of something although I am conscious, and these are in fact answers to rather different questions.

WADDINGTON

Do you think you can be conscious, but conscious of nothing?

LUCAS

It is a state which some of my pupils are in. Can I pick up one other point — I thought that at one stage you were carefully demolishing the arguments, which seemed to me to be very good, for describing consciousness or the capacity for having experience at least, to animals. Having knocked this down, you then suddenly turned your agnosticism upside down, and imputed consciousness to the sticks and stones which Tony laughed at you last time for doing.

WADDINGTON

That was the paradox I was trying to bring out.

LUCAS

But I think this is a paradox.

WADDINGTON

Yes.

KENNY

I think there was also another paradox, wasn't there? The other night you were suggesting that Christopher and I had been mistaken in concentrating so much on language, and that there were beings who had minds even though they didn't have language — namely, dumb animals, who you said have minds because they are conscious.

WADDINGTON

No, I didn't say 'because they were conscious'. I said they had minds, but it wasn't because I knew they were conscious.

KENNY

So you do know they have minds, but you aren't sure whether they are conscious? But then what is the ground for saying with certainty that they have minds, if you think it is a dubitable hypothesis that they have consciousness?

WADDINGTON

Because I use 'mind' to refer to a highly complex neural interrelation. If I see a thing behaving in a very complicated way — if I see a cat watch a mouse go down a hole and I know that the hole goes round a corner, and comes out over there, and the cat goes over there to wait for the mouse, I say it's got a mind. But whether it is conscious or not I can't tell — it probably is conscious, but I don't really ask the question 'is it conscious or not?'. But if I do ask that question, I come to the conclusion that sticks and stones must be in some sense conscious too. I ask if an animal has got a mind, in the sense of: is its behaviour a complex pattern?

145

LONGUET-HIGGINS

But we do know about cats that they can actually remember what happened yesterday. And dogs can certainly remember smells, and so forth. And we have no reason to suppose that sticks and stones can. So there's good evidence, it seems to me, for consciousness — as opposed to walking in one's sleep, as it were — as far as cats go, but no evidence whatever as far as sticks and stones go.

WADDINGTON

Well, is it evidence for consciousness? It's evidence for their behaviour — that it is modified by something that happened yesterday.

LONGUET-HIGGINS

You mean that they were in a learning situation yesterday?

WADDINGTON

Yes. They were in a learning situation yesterday, and today they remember. But that does not involve using the word 'remember' in the sense in which it means that you can call up a mental picture in consciousness. I'm saying that all you can say is that the animal's behaviour today is modified by what happened to its nervous system yesterday.

LUCAS

That's not all you can say. This is your *evidence*, but it doesn't seem to me that it is all you can *say*, because if this were all that you could say, then you would take the position that Descartes took, that there is no reason whatever for objecting to vivisection, and one should no more complain of this cat screaming as you degutted it, than you feel sorry for the car when you clash the gears.

WADDINGTON

No; I think, as I said, that they probably are conscious, but I don't reckon that I can get any definite evidence of it. But in the absence of definite evidence against it, I would prefer to operate on the basis that they presumably are.

LONGUET-HIGGINS

But what's wrong with this definition of consciousness as opposed to self-consciousness, that one has a memory and that one is putting things into it at a particular time?

WADDINGTON

Well, computers have memory stores that beat mine absolutely hollow, but —

LONGUET-HIGGINS

Well would this not do as a definition of *that* sort of consciousness?

WADDINGTON

Just because you've got a memory store, made of whatever it is made of doesn't show you are conscious in any sense of the word that —

LONGUET-HIGGINS

Well, put it this way: couldn't we use a different word for

146

having a learning capacity and a memory? There's nothing about sticks and stones which gives us the slightest reason for supposing that they have learning capacity and memory. So I think that there are no good grounds for –

WADDINGTON

For saying that these things have *minds*. Capacities don't really apply – They probably are conscious, but I don't know.

KENNY

When do you think they are even probably conscious? I mean, if consciousness is something so much beyond the reach of evidence, why can you go even as far as a probability?

WADDINGTON

Because it's absolutely within the reach of evidence in myself. I am clear that I –

KENNY

But isn't it very rash to generalise from a single case like that?

WADDINGTON

There's only one earth, but nobody would say you can't generalise about things on earth because there's only one of it. Of course you can generalise from a single case.

KENNY

But the parallel generalisation would be to say that every planet is inhabited. Of course, we only happen to know that one of them is inhabited, but why shouldn't the others all be like this? That is the parallel between saying 'Your body is conscious, therefore every body is conscious'.

LONGUET-HIGGINS

But surely you would agree that there's a difference between the concept of consciousness as you've been using it, and the concept of self-consciousness?

WADDINGTON

Yes, yes, I would agree there's a difference in that. You can be perfectly conscious and it's only quite rarely that you are self-conscious. I wouldn't put it past some people never to be self-conscious.

Language and Thought

KENNY

I want to follow on from what Waddington has been saying. What he said this evening showed that I misunderstood him in thinking that he was equating consciousness and mind, but it has made it clear to me that I wasn't mistaken in attributing to him the belief in this essentially private entity to which only he had access. Only I was mistaken in thinking that he called it 'mind', when in fact he calls it 'consciousness'. And I have been arguing that the notion of this essentially private entity is a mythical one. I don't want to go over the arguments for that again, but rather to try to bring out the relationship between the issue of privacy and the issue of language.

147

I think that Longuet-Higgins and I both attribute a greater importance to language for the study of mind than our two other colleagues. And we have been attacked for this in different ways by Waddington and Lucas. But I think that John, at least, in his paper the other night, tended to identify the issue of privacy versus publicity with the issue of language versus non-language. The horror story about the person suffering in the operation and unable to express his pain, was of course meant as an argument against the privacy of sensation and it was not – or I can't see how it was – an argument against the language-dependent nature of mind. I've said that I don't want to go over the privacy argument again, but I would like to develop a bit the argument about the relationship between language and thought. I've said that many thoughts, indeed all the thoughts which are particularly characteristic of human beings (as distinct from the thought that there's a mouse in the corner or the thought that it's about time that that can of dog food was opened, which are thoughts that might be attributed to animals) are thoughts which it is inconceivable that somebody can have unless he has the use of language. I don't want to say that every thought is, as it were, formed in the mind, in impeccable sentences, or is even verbalised at all – what I do want to say is that the criterion of identity for thoughts, that is to say, how you specify what a particular thought is, how you tell one thought from another thought, is given by the expression of thoughts in words.

We symposiasts in these meetings have been trying to communicate thoughts. What we have given you, of course, has been words. But the words aren't just a surrogate for thoughts. In communicating the words we do communicate the thoughts, and until we have the words the thoughts – those particular thoughts – are not quite clear to ourselves either. Any expression of a thought which I can give to myself I can give to you too. And this is the way in which the issue of privacy does connect with the issue of language, because of the public nature of language. There are, of course, thoughts which flash through our minds, as I said yesterday, which are not at all verbalised. But the example that I gave yesterday was meant simply to illustrate the modest claim that it was possible to have a thought which was not verbalised which nonetheless was a thought which only a language-user could have. And so most of the evidence which has been brought by people in these meetings and at the reception last night, showing that there can be unverbalised thoughts, was not to the point, was not a counter-example to the claim about the language-dependentness of thought, because the simple example I gave showed that there can be unverbalised thoughts which nonetheless only a language-user could have.

I said that the criterion of identity for thoughts was their expression in language. If you want to know what thoughts are going through somebody's mind, even your own mind, you can only express them, you can only nail down the thought as that particular thought, by giving it expression in language. Of course, one's relation to one's own thoughts is different from one's relation to other people's thoughts, because the onus of expressing the thought and the capacity to express the thought, belongs to me in the case of my own thoughts, whereas for other people it is how they express the thoughts that decide what the thought is.

I have said that if I communicate the right words to you, I am genuinely communicating my thoughts. And against Waddington I would say I can also communicate my experiences. He said, 'I can only communicate *about* my experiences — I can't communicate my experiences'. But to communicate an experience precisely *is* to describe it to somebody else. What he had in mind was sharing an experience in the sense in which two people would have the same experience. Now in the perfectly natural sense of having the same experience, of course, two people can have the same experience. Whatever the experience he was having when he was looking at his paper, I could have it too if I got into the same place and looked at the paper as well. What he meant was, I think, not this natural sense of having the same experience, but he meant we couldn't have *numerically the same* experience. And he argued from that that experiences are somehow essentially private. I don't think the argument works. We can't have numerically the same nose, because the nose I have is my nose, and the nose he has is his nose, but this doesn't mean that noses are essentially private objects.

LUCAS

I want to protest at one point. There seem to be two Kenny theses — one is one which is true, that all human beings that we ever come into contact with are language-users, and therefore all the difficult thoughts that we are concerned with, not only the Thistle Freezers, but many others, are in fact possessed by people who have the use of language and if they didn't have the use of language they wouldn't be in the position to come to Edinburgh and see about Thistle Freezers. But this could be guyed, I think, by another point, that it is inconceivable, we could say, that there could be someone who has these high-grade thoughts unless he's been fed. One might start using a sort of low-grade argument for High Tables — that Oxford dons don't think unless they have a proper intake of calories. And then you could say, much more importantly, that of course people always have parents. And there are a whole lot of other things, and these are important truths, but they don't really define the nature of thought. And then there was a shift: as soon as he'd said this point, which is true but

149

not relevant, Tony then said something about the criterion of identity – how you specify. Well, of course, if I am asked to specify, I must use language. I can't answer his questions without using words. But I still protest that there is something, that people do have thoughts. I remember – it's just come to my mind this moment – that Beethoven, I think in one of his letters, says that he can't say what is in his mind; but if only the person was here to listen to a tune, that would express it.

LONGUET-HIGGINS

If I understand Tony Kenny, he attaches special importance to language because it is a symbolic representation of our mental processes. But the same could be said of music, and I would insist that one could think in music, and I imagine Tony would have allowed that to be included. But I do, I think, take issue with him on Waddington's cat, and that mouse-hole, because I am deeply impressed by Waddington's cat. It obviously thinks – we can express in words what it is thinking: 'That mouse has gone into that hole; that hole goes up to that point there; I will go to that point' – and it jolly well does. Surely that is thought, although it is not linguistically expressible by the cat. And so I feel myself out of sympathy with you on that point.

KENNY

No, I entirely agree with you, that the cat can have that sort of thought, and in a rather complicated sentence I tried to exclude that sort of thought from the type of thought which I was claiming could only be expressed in language. What I should say is that I think that all thoughts are expressible. There are some thoughts, like thoughts about mice and holes, that are expressible in non-linguistic behaviour, but there are also many thoughts, such as all the thoughts that we've heard in this room during the Gifford Lectures, which are only expressible in linguistic behaviour. What I'm against are the entirely inexpressible thoughts that John thinks are the really important things.

With regard to John's comparison with the importance of being fed in order to think, I do believe that the impossibility of having thoughts about philosophy, say, without language, is an inconceivability. It doesn't seem to me inconceivable that there can be thoughts without there being food. As John indeed knows, I, unlike him, think that it is not inconceivable that computers have thoughts. But computers, unlike Oxford dons, don't need to live at High Table.

WADDINGTON

May I take up a point which Christopher rather casually threw out. Language is only a symbolic description of situations. Now this was an important point – I really was not the slightest convinced by Tony when he compared his nose to my piece of paper, at the end of his talk. The point I was trying to make is that you can send things from one person to another, including pieces of paper, and including noses – it's not so often done with noses, but you do get people giving each other their hearts. And these are perfectly transferable. But you cannot transfer my experience of the piece of chalk or the piece of paper. It is, I think, private in a way that a nose or a heart is certainly not private, if you let yourself get into the hands of a surgeon.

KENNY

We can only one of us have the nose at the same time, and it is that sort of thing that is the parallel with the experience.

Reflection

LUCAS

'Reflexivity', I should have written down. I am going to toss the ball first, I think, in the direction of Christopher Longuet-Higgins. Going back to our fifth lecture, when he tried to stymie me in the conversation, by putting the question 'Would a rational being fail to answer this question in the affirmative?' And he thought this would catch me on the horns of a dilemma. Would a rational being (that's who I'm supposed to identify with) fail to answer this question, thereby showing himself not to be rational? Or would he say 'yes', thereby saying that he is not rational. (See pp. 67–8.) And I escaped from that dilemma by claiming that there was a loop in it. 'Would a rational being fail to answer this question?' And that is where you say 'What?' and force the computer, or whatever it was on Forrest Hill, back to say it again – 'Would a rational being . . .' And later on it turned up in our later discussions, that there is a danger of a programme ending up in a loop, and he didn't quite like to ban all such things as being true or false, or as feasible or non-feasible, but said there was some problem here. And I think there is. And the reason why I first of all want to wear a slight white sheet is that although in this question there does seem to me to be a loop, there are some other self-referring statements, or self-referring questions, where there doesn't seem to be anything terribly wrong. 'Is this an English sentence?' – we don't seem to find that unintelligible. And what I'm not at all clear about at the moment, is where we do and where we do not get these apparent vicious circles. Some sentences that we can find in some formal languages are ones such that we can get a perfectly good recursive class of them, and others not. And I want to throw this open really, for him to pick up. It is relevant not only because it lies near the core of my Gödelian argument, but because, as we were arguing a day or two ago, there seems to be some parallel about the ability of a mind to reflect on itself. That is, it is because a mind can reflect on itself that we get leverage for Gödel's theorem. It's because a mind can reflect on itself that we get all sorts of problems about the nature of mind. One coming up only this evening, the possible distinction between consciousness and self-consciousness.

Well, I'll throw this first of all to Longuet-Higgins.

LONGUET-HIGGINS

Well, plainly, reflexivity is a characteristic of natural language. I think we would all agree, unless we were particularly pernickety, that 'Is this an English question?' is in fact a well-formed English question, with a perfectly clear meaning, and that the question should be answered in the affirmative. I think there's no doubt in anybody's mind that that is alright. The possibility of the sentences of the language — sorry, let me put it at the semantic level, — statements of the language referring to statements in the language, including themselves, or others which refer back to them, is something which is obviously characteristic of human language. It is also a characteristic of human thought. It raises problems. It means that if we think of utterances in natural languages, as I would like to think of them, as equivalent to programs which we write to one another, then those programs can have loops in them. And it's because a program can have a loop in it that some English sentences are in fact never going to be fully capable of elucidation. This really makes perfectly good sense. If you think of sentences in natural language as equivalent to pieces of program for a computer, some programs do have loops, but that doesn't mean that programming languages are silly, and it doesn't mean that computers are irrational, and it doesn't mean, I think — applying it to ourselves — that we are irrational or silly or that our language is silly. It's only when we approach language in the wrong way — when we treat English, for example, as an indicative language — that we really get into trouble. That was the burden of my song when I was contrasting the semantics of indicative languages, where you have the Tarski trouble, with the semantics of English, where I think you are really dealing with an imperative language.

KENNY

I wanted to follow up Christopher's objection to John on this line. You remember that John Lucas argued that minds were not machines because, given any machine working algorithmically, we could produce something which would be like a Gödelian formula, that is to say, we could present it with a formula which we could see to be true, but the machine couldn't prove to be true. When John first produced this argument, one of his critics, I think it was Professor Whiteley, made the following objection: he said "Take this sentence: 'John Lucas cannot consistently make this judgment'." Now, he said, clearly any other human being except John Lucas can see that this is true, without inconsistency. But clearly John can't make this judgment without inconsistency, therefore that

152

shows that we all have a property which he doesn't have, which makes us as much superior to him as we all are to computers. And I wonder what his answer was to that.

LUCAS

Well, I will answer that. People always want to see me locked in battle with a computer, each of us trying to get the upper hand. And I have a much more modest ambition: I just want to show that we are different. And of course it is absolutely true – I do concede that other people are superior to me, and one of their very reasons is that they are other. But what that sentence shows is that other people are other – and I don't think even Dr Kenny would deny that.

I still feel that I ought to be a bit more unhappy about this, and the reason is that there is some criterion of what does and does not count as self-reference, which has eluded me. The simple solution which I was using here, seems to me to be a bit too strong – it's rather like the solution which was proposed in mathematics after Russell's Paradox emerged, where we ban all of those classes which are defined in terms of themselves. And one throws all the impredicable sets out of the window. And then one has a very great task in reconstructing mathematics, without any impredicable definitions at all. And this seems to me to be too stringent. I want to get something slightly more relaxed, which will discriminate between those entirely acceptable in predicable definitions, – where it is perfectly reasonable to say 'of course I know what sentence he is making, of course I know what question he is asking', and I would just simply be rude or silly if I keep on interrupting him after the word 'this' or the word 'question' – and other cases – where there does seem to be some very substantial point at issue. This is something which is I think really more a matter of mathematical logic, where I rather hope that Christopher will come up with more things, because is seems to me to arise in the imperative as well as in the indicative mood. But I don't think this is just simply a matter of mathematical logic. It does seem to me that one of the characteristic features of the mind is its ability to reflect on itself, and this is why we keep on running into a whole series of difficulties. We get into the paradoxes which I mentioned, I think two nights ago, that if I am going to regard myself as a mind I am not only conscious but I am conscious that I am conscious. Not only can I think but I can think of my thinking. And there is a sort of certain infinite capacity of the mind which parallels the infinity of the natural numbers, and is the reason why one can, in the case of – do you want to interrupt, Professor Longuet-Higgins?

LONGUET-HIGGINS

Well, yes, I would like to make a point here. There's something which is very difficult to do, but I think that most computer scientists reckon that it will be done with success before very long, That is, to write programs which can study themselves. There's no reason to imagine that this is beyond the reach of ingenious programming, but until we have that kind of thing, you would be quite right to say that we definitely have the edge over the computers! But I would also like to say something else. You won a very good debating point against Tony just a moment ago, in saying that the Gödel argument shows that he is 'other', or that you are 'other'. But I don't think that's quite how you use the argument in your book. You were rather suggesting that there was some superiority attached to human beings because they could always out-Gödel a machine, but, by implication, but never explicitly, a machine could never out-Gödel them. But actually I could write a program to print out that question to you, and that would out-Gödel you. And so we can't easily conclude from this style of argument anything very interesting about the mind.

KENNY

Well, now he's withdrawn even further from his original position, making the difference between men and computers only like the difference between one man and the next man, one computer and the next computer.

LUCAS

This is enough, though — if I am as unlike any computer as I am unlike Kenny, then I can be sure that I am what I always thought I was. I think self-reflection is not only a characteristic of mind; it is one that can be taken in a rather grandiloquent or perhaps a rather more humble way. If I remember rightly, Aristotle also saw the ability to reflect on oneself as a characteristic of mental power, and in fact he went further, and said that it was the peculiar activity of the Aristotelian God that he should spend his time thinking about his own excellence. Now I think there are objections to this, on good Christian doctrinal grounds, as well as those of natural theology, but the terms of Adam Gifford's bequest prevent me basing any argument on revealed religion, and I shall leave it for a later occasion to try and see more fully what is wrong with this on grounds of logic alone. This will need further researches by Longuet-Higgins. But for the moment I think we should draw just this one alternative conclusion, and that is not to think that it is a mark of the mind as exemplified in God to reflect upon its own perfection, but rather with us it is a characteristic feature of the mind that it enables men to reflect on their own imperfections, both in their thinking and in their doing.

Index of Names